D1314625

A DECADE

OF

RURAL PROGRESS

Based on:

Reports of Committees to the American Country Life Association.

The Proceedings of the Tenth National Country Life Conference, East Lansing, Michigan, August 1-4, 1927.

The Proceedings of the Eleventh National Country Life Conference, Urbana, Illinois, June 19-21, 1928.

Edited by
BENSON Y. LANDIS
and
NAT T. FRAME

PUBLISHED BY
THE UNIVERSITY OF CHICAGO PRESS
FOR THE
AMERICAN COUNTRY LIFE ASSOCIATION
Waddington Farm, Wheeling, W. Va.

Composed and Printed by
THE OWL PRINT SHOP
Wheeling, W. Va.
U. S. A.

CONTENTS

PART I. THE ISSUES IN RURAL PROGRESS

PART II. A DECADE OF RURAL PROGRESS

PART I.   THE ISSUES IN RURAL PROGRESS

(a)   The Issues of Farm Life, By Kenyon L. Butterfield.

(b)   Suggestions Regarding Emphases, By Liberty Hyde Bailey.

(c)   Some Aspects of the Agricultural Situation, By William M. Jardine.

(d)   Science in Rural Human Relationships, By Charles J. Galpin.

A DECADE OF RURAL PROGRESS

THE ISSUES OF FARM LIFE*

KENYON L. BUTTERFIELD
President, American Country Life Association

Since the dawn of his intelligence, man has struggled for a livelihood. He has used various tools—tools of wood, tools of stone, tools of iron. Through the centuries he has gained an increased mastery of nature's forces and materials. But the struggle for livelihood still goes on under new forms, and will go on indefinitely.

Gradually, however, there emerged the quest for the personal development of the individual. This urge for the growth of the human spirit became a great goal for humanity, and finally resulted not only in the ideals that make civilization,—such as individual freedom, dignity of personality, and religion, but led to the most vital ideal of all, that which was embodied in the life and teachings of the Master.

Today in America the energies and skill of mankind, working on marvelous material resources, have produced a physical civilization and a distributed comfort beyond all the dreams of olden days.

But this material development, which has gone on all over the world to a lesser degree than with us, has brought an entirely new moral problem. Of old, the moral question was, how can men reach their full stature in poverty? That is still a question. But in America, another question arises, how can people reach their full stature morally and spiritually in prosperity? This statement does not assume that all Americans are prosperous. There are enormously wide discrepancies in wealth, there are still people living from hand to mouth. At the same time, in no country today, and at no time in the world's history, has there been so much of prosperity, so many items of comfort and convenience as here in America.

It may be said, therefore, that the modern world on the moral side faces the question of human development under terms both of adversity and of prosperity, of poverty and of wealth, of deprivation and of plenty, and of all the grades in between these extremes.

*From Address at Tenth National Country Life Conference.

7

Generally speaking, the tiller of the soil all through history has been an underling. There have been notable exceptions, as in the palmy days of the Roman republic, two or three centuries ago when the yoemen of England were in power, today in a country like Denmark; but the greatest exception on a large scale has probably been the American farmer. From the standpoint of intelligence, of economic independence, and of opportunity for the rural youth to leave his class, the American farmer has been and probably still is the greatest exception.

In recent years and particularly in the last decade, the enormous development of industry and of commerce through the application of science, the standardization of manufacture, the remarkable organization of business and its immense capitalization, have especially, in America, ushered in an entirely new chapter of relationship between rural and urban. For along side of this new business development has come a depressed agriculture very difficult to explain, very complex, but very real.

Now out of this situation there arises at least three great issues that are of the utmost significance in rural affairs and that promise to affect our entire civilization.

First of all, is the fundamental economic question, how can a body of farmers be retained upon American soil, who are economically efficient and free, and who can compete with industry and commerce for capital, for labor, and for income or standard of living.

Secondly, there is the even more fundamental question whether the quality of the people on the land can be kept upon a par with an urban civilization that commands such enormous resources for education and the development of social institutions of various sorts.

And then deeper than all, is the question common to all mankind, both in city and in country, how character building can be advanced in a world dominated by enormous activity of an economic sort. This is an abiding issue in any civilization, but it takes on a new significance today, because of the new problems that arise out of an industrial and urban development so rapid and so powerful that it seems at times to be beyond human control.

It is not within the capacity of any one man to indicate the solution of these problems, but a few aims or goals may perhaps be suggested.

(1)   In the first place, there must be a general recognition on the part of all our people that the rural problem is present and significant, and that it is of quite a much concern to the cities as to the country side itself.

(2)   That the conditions under which farmers work are such that probably agriculture will have to be made "a most favored industry." In the activities of industrial and commercial organizations, as well as in such legislation as may be necessary to direct economic tendencies, agriculture must be regarded as a first consideration. Unless this is done, it is almost certain that urban and industrial self interest will crowd agriculture to the wall, until such time as the same self interest comes to a realization that not only the maintenance of an adequate food supply, but the maintenance of a high type of people on the soil, is an essential of the common problem of world civilization.

(3)   It must be recognized also that urban wealth must help support rural institutions,—roads, schools, hospitals, churches, not merely as a matter of philanthropy, but chiefly on the principle that the total social wealth must be utilized for total social health. The education, the intelligence, the satisfying life in the small village or the open country, is just as legitimate a charge upon urban industry and trade as is the development of highly favored institutions in the city.

(4)   In the next place, the farmers themselves must be organized and encouraged to organize; and this not merely in self defense, although that is probably vital under present conditions of human society. This organization will take many forms, but primarily it will have three major aspects: (a) the thorough-going organization of the men interested in a given commodity, such as wheat or milk, and the bringing to bear on the problems of this commodity the scientific as well as the organized forces that are available. (b) the organization of the local or town and country community, which must be developed to its fullest capacity through the intelligent activity of its members if we are to have an adequate rural civilization.

(c)   And in the third place, a general associated organization of farmers, that may for want of a better term be called political, although not political in the ordinary sense of the word. But it is to have the task of mobilizing the intelligence, the moral power, and the activity of rural folk on behalf of both their own interests and of the common interests of this country and of all mankind.

Farmers of course have reciprocal duties. They have an obligation to society to be efficient in the use of the land and in the maintenance of soil resources. They have an obligation to utilize modern social institutions such as school and library and church and hospital. And, while the city must recognize the right and desirability of the farmers to organize, the farmers themselves must use their organization quite as much for the common good as for class interest.

But above all, let us not forget that, while the present day world is at work—subduing nature, utilizing material resources, building the huge machinery of civilization—the abiding issues of farm life, as of all life, lie after all in the subordination of the material to the spiritual, of the physical to the moral. In other words, they lie in such principles as the supreme worth of the individual, the giving of each individual both the opportunity and the stimulus for the maximum development of his mind and spirit, and the cooperation of individuals, of families, of communities, of states, of nations, of races, for the common welfare of all mankind.

SUGGESTIONS REGARDING EMPHASES*

Liberty Hyde Bailey

Chairman of the Country Life Commission Appointed By President Roosevelt

I have been impressed for many years that if we make mistakes in our country life work the major ones are not in our reports. They are not in our findings. They are not in our intentions. They are in the emphasis that we place on certain facts, certain points of view, certain positions.

So I am minded to say something about the dangers of over-emphasis of certain phases of country life work. First, be careful of dissatisfactions. Within the last generation we have bred a race of professional dissatisfiers, and I very much fear that we are in danger of breeding something of the kind in country life work, and if we do it will be the greatest calamity that can overtake agriculture.

In the second place, I think we have made a mistake in supposing that the plight of the farmer is merely necessitous.

In the third place, we must not suppose that all farmers can be made prosperous and contented. It cannot be accomplished, and there are two main reasons why it cannot be accomplished. The character of the man has so much to do with it. We have been in the process now for about two generations of sorting out the rural population. The sorting process is not yet complete.

Not all the soils and places where the farms are located are adapted to farming. There are many parts of this country in which farmers ought not to live in the sense of trying to till their land and to make a living from it. One of the great economic and political problems of the future is to redistribute the farming population. I have recently had occasion to make some suggestions whereby this may or may not be accomplished.

And, again, people in general overstress the relative importance of the economic situation. We are measuring farming by economics. Now bear in mind that I am making no comparison with the great science of economics which must make a vaster contribution than in the direct realms of commerce and trade. We made a mistake by

*From Address at Tenth National Country Life Conference.

supposing that the commercial valuations are the principal indices of the rural situation. I am not sure that the fundamental theory of much of our commercial economics is sound.

And there is a following among us who if they would not measure the rural situation by the commercial economic yardstick would measure it by the social group, and I think they are as far wrong as the other, in the very fact that they are so likely to work with groups and not with persons. Civilization is a biological phenomenon. Rural life is only one phase of it. It must rest directly upon the welfare of the individual; the contentment, the activity, and the peace of mind of that individual.

We are likely to overstress the significance of what we now call welfare, which has come to be a semi-professional and semi-technical term. And welfare associates itself very largely with groups and with surveys. And just so far as it forgets the welfare of the individual person, of John and Mary and Jane and Henry, just so far does it fail of making its greatest contribution. Democracy is by no means the covering up of the individual in the mass. Rather the building upon the individual and giving him larger liberty and expression as a part of the body politic. You must never forget the individual soul.

We are likely to overstress the idea of training for leadership, as if leadership were itself a profession comparable with law or medicine. But leadership is the natural result of the fruition of an effective and good life.

We are likely relatively to overvalue the farmer's production as his contribution to society, the commodities that he raises and provides for the market. His best contribution immediately is himself and his family. Or if you want to look objectively and with the long view as to the interests of society, his chief contribution is to maintain the earth fit for human habitation, beautiful and fertile. And he is the keeper of it now as he was in the beginning.

I fear we are in danger of losing something of our ideal, sacrificing it to expertness. Expert knowledge can never take the place of spiritual outlook. Of course, we have passed the early days of country life work when it was a gospel to us, when there was so much of the missionary spirit; when there was the uplift; when there was the eagerness everywhere to work every hour in the day in which we could be awake for the good of those folk there.

We have written much, I more than my share. We have written much about the possibilities of country life. Here the farming people are set against the best background that the earth affords, and we have not yet capitalized it or made it real to them.

I think we must get back to the man and the woman. I know that you are doing it, but I think that idea must be emphasized more the country over, not in any spirit of uplift on the part of the workers. We had to combat that all the way across the continent back and forth in the days of the old Country Life Commission and at every hearing had to explain, as Dr. Butterfield well remembers, that it was not an uplift enterprise, not a superimposed structure. In other words, I think the real country life movement, when it shall have completely found itself and made itself felt, will be a religious movement in the best and divinest sense.

And, lastly, let me say that we are too ready to measure all the elements of the rural situation in terms of our present day standards. Farming is as old as the hills. We are trying to solve it by twentieth century criteria. No wonder we fail. By what other standards can we solve it? I do not know. I only wish to drop into your minds the thought that we are not to solve these difficulties today or tomorrow. Milton said, "They also serve who only stand and wait."

From the dawn of history, men have been farmers of one kind or another through all the mists of the centuries, and through all their wanderings over the earth they have taken to a piece of land and lived on it. Like the birds and animals, in a way, they have become a part of the environment, and adapted to a natural situation. That situation is not easily changed. We have only begun working at these problems. This society is only ten years old. The Commission of Country Life was organized in 1908.

We have been working at this problem how long, consciously— not yet twenty-five years. What is twenty-five years in the running of the centuries in which this great fundamental vocation of mankind has been settling itself over the face of the earth and sending its roots deep into the verities of life? Can you change it in a generation? Can you change it in a generation of investigation and philosophy and prospect? It might be likened to a great river which takes its source back in the hills, flows down across the piedmont and plains and into the seas by several fingering mouths. Men build their little wharves at various points and send their little ships of the ideas far away, not knowing whither they go. But the river always moves and joins the background with the sea.

The picture of the situation is one to give us pause. I commend every piece of work that every one of you is doing. It will all be a contribution to the final result. The synthesis has not yet come. The big movements have not yet been visioned.

SOME ASPECTS OF THE AGRICULTURAL SITUATION*

WILLIAM M. JARDINE
Secretary of Agriculture

A representative survey just completed by the Department of Agriculture indicates that 84 per cent of the farmers who moved to towns between 1917 and 1926 owned their farms at the time the change was made. No doubt many of these farms were mortgaged. The families included in this survey had lived from one to more than forty years on the farms from which they moved. Those who were classed as owners had been in actual possession of farms from a year to more than half a century. The majority of the farmers included in the survey operated over 100 acres each. More than half of the farmers were under 50 years of age.

They gave as their reasons for leaving the farms: Economic, 37.8 per cent; old age and physical disabilities, 25.2 per cent; opportunity to give children better schooling, 10.9 per cent; because of having achieved a competency, 2.5 per cent; in order to let son have farm, 1.8 per cent; all other reasons, 21.8 per cent.

A certain part of this movement is due to the natural long-time adjustment which will always go on between industrial and agricultural activities and methods of earning a livelihood. It is a healthy movement. It need not operate to the disadvantage of agriculture.

So long as we have adequate production, our main interest is not in reducing numerically the movement from farms to cities. Rather, our problem is to keep on the farm those men and women who know rural life, who love it, and who can contribute substantially to its development.

Many of the factors which tend to make the farm seem less attractive than the city can be controlled. I have had a great deal to say in the past, and I shall have more to say in the future, regarding the necessity of gaining for agriculture its proper economic status—its proper share of our national income. It is obvious that many people do leave the farms because they feel they can make the move to their

From Address at Tenth National Country Life Conference.

14

own economic advantage. The economic aspects of farming have been so thoroughly and sincerely studied that from all our efforts must come some sound solution to the problem of making the economic reward of rural endeavor as great as that of city endeavor.

Obviously, however, many of those who leave the farms—and not a few of them are highly competent—are moving to town to give their children and themselves the benefits of the city's standard of living. What happens when a fairly well-to-do farmer moves to the city? He either sells his farm or places a tenant in charge. If the latter occurs, the farm must then support two families. The new man, as a general rule, has his fortune to make out of the soil. The prosperous farmer takes to the city with him his years of experience and education in business-like farming, his wealth which was produced on the land, and his desire to live a more comfortable life. The rural neighborhood, school, club, church, and local government lose a substantial supporter. Even if he retains ownership of the farm, his income from the land is usually spent in the city. Should he sell the farm outright, that wealth goes to build up the city and its business. By remaining on the farm, the fairly well-to-do man could do much to raise the standard of living in his community. In moving to the city, he enters an entirely new environment with a good chance of being a misfit in the new surroundings.

Only a month ago I visited several farms in Kansas. For thirty years Mr. Taylor and his family have lived on a 160-acre piece of land in the central part of the State. Taylor himself has retired; but he continues to live on the farm; his sons are in charge of its actual operation. The farm home has a small, but good library. There are a fireplace, a radio, and a piano. Shrubs and trees shade and beautify the home. The house, pump house, and barn are equipped with electricity. There is running water in the house. Mr. Taylor has even laid out a nine-hole golf course on a hilly section of his land; that particular piece of land is grazed by sheep. All that Mr. Taylor and his family have was made from the land. That wealth has been invested right at home. His family is benefited. The entire community is benefited.

Just across the road is another farm. Its soil is as rich and as productive as Mr. Taylor's farm. Ten years ago its owner felt that he had sufficient money to move to town. He placed a tenant in charge. Today the foundation on that farm home is rotting. There are few trees and no shrubs. The land produces bountifully, but the income seeps to the city. Ten years ago the farm offered better living conditions than it does today.

The perennial loss of surplus wealth is one of the outstanding causes of a barren country life. Amazing slow of accumulation, surplus wealth can do much when wisely utilized.   Surplus wealth in a nation is the means of culture, civilization.

I want to emphasize that included among the people who are moving from the farms are many who could readily remain, who could make a real contribution to rural life, and who would be genuinely happy in a good rural environment.   These people are leaving the country partly because we are not emphasizing in a big enough way the real advantages of rural life, partly because we have not made the American countryside what we ought to make it.   We too often think of the open country merely as trade territory tributary to cities and towns.   We have not enough concern with it as a living element in our national life.   We go on draining the country, the source of much of our spiritual as well as economic resources, and we are putting very little back.

Manifestly we are not so much concerned with what has occurred in the past—except for the lessons it has taught us—as we are in the prospects for the immediate future and the distant future.   Certainly the farmer wants culture for his family, education, recreation, entertainment, health facilities close at hand, art in public buildings, comfort and beauty in homes.   The farmer, poor or prosperous, wants these things.

As I see it, if we are to develop a fuller and richer rural life, if we are to make farm life and the farm home sufficiently attractive to keep the best farmers in the rural communities, we must pay more attention to the technical principles of rural consumption.   That is to say, we must assist the rural communities to achieve the highest possible standard of living on their income.   It will be to the distinct advantage of every individual and to the American Nation as a whole to achieve efficiency in rural consumption.

The Government has the legal authority to assist in research and educational work directed toward the development of rural life and the rural home.   The Department of Agriculture stands firmly behind the promotion of such a program.   Cities have technical experts in many lines of living who work out the principles of consumption on a high level for the masses.   Individuals in cities do not work out these problems for themselves even though they have the money to pay for a high standard of living.   The masses depend on an army of experts in many phases of health, architecture, sanitation, public utilities, municipal government, education, information, play, art, religion.   The farmer has few, if any, of these experts and he can not individually draw experts to his aid.

The farmer needs expert assistance—just as city people need expert assistance—in working out the principles of consumption.   This need is on the same level as the need for expert assistance in the principles of production and marketing.

A plan to equip the country with the institutions of health and culture and facilities for education and entertainment deserves an application of brain power co-equal with the brain power applied through agricultural colleges and governmental agencies to achieve on the farm more efficient production and greater financial returns. The people of this country have been liberal in providing funds for the latter type of work. Is it not of equal importance that we develop an effective program, properly financed, to get for the farmer those facilities for education, recreation, entertainment, that he desires?

We can make the country so attractive that the farmer, upon becoming well off, will not want to leave the farm. Rural America has so many natural advantages over city life that the raising of its standard of living should be urged to the utmost. When I see children growing up on the crowded quarters of cities and playing in traffic jammed streets, I can not but think of the opportunity for physical and mental development in the country where children can play in the open and live in contact with nature's plant and animal life. Oh, no, the rural side of the picture isn't all dark. Every family has a house, literally bathed in sunshine, with plenty of space inside and out for children to grow in. And the children are there, too, using this sunshine, air, and space. In America, more than half the people on farms are children. To be exact, 50.4 per cent of the population are under twenty-one. In the cities, only 37.5 per cent of the population are under twenty-one. The country is the home of children.

But it takes more than fresh air and the songs of birds to build the type of rural civilization we all want. It takes rural statesmanship and cooperative self-help on the part of farmers themselves. This calls for more than high-sounding essays. It demands constructive national policies. It means that we must keep in the country more of those leaders who can contribute to the building up of our rural civilization. Some of America's greatest statesmen, financiers, leaders have come from the country. Some of our dearest traditions are centered in the rural communities. The country will always be the source of this inspiration and this leadership, but we must not rob rural life of its leadership to too great an extent. We must keep a great deal of it there to build, bit by bit, until our rural countryside has all the things which now attract many farmers to the city.

SCIENCE IN RURAL HUMAN RELATIONSHIPS*

C. J. GALPIN

Division of Farm Population and Rural Life Studies,
United States Department of Agriculture

The last ten years of rural life in the United States, occupying the foreground of our picture tonight, melt by insensible degrees into a background of more than 200 years of rural life history. Decade by decade, you see the percentage decline of the rural population and the corresponding increase of the urban, until in 1920 it is found that less than half the total population is rural and major part of our population is urban. I am inclined to consider the 200-year period of rural life from 1710 to 1910 as one block of rural life history; and to characterize it broadly; and briefly to evaluate its meaning to American national life. Then I propose to take the collapse in the growth of the farm population beginning in 1910 and continuing to 1927 as a significant index of a transition,—in fact, a transition marking a crisis in rural life history. Within this period of transition and crisis the last ten-year span, 1917-1927, stands forth shining with the spot light upon it.

What I especially perceive in the rural life of this first 200 years is an amazing psychology of freedom, induced by contacts without restraint with the great spaces of plains, mountains, valleys, forests. This unrestricted freedom and boundless autonomy of the pioneer created virility, unreflecting self confidence, and high imagination. And the debt of the nation to the rural life of this first period is for a constant inoculation of the growing cities with the serum of imaginative youth from the farms.

There then is the frame and the background of the picture of American rural progress. In the foreground very intimate to us is a close-up of ten years. This tiny span finds itself in a different period,— a period of paradox with loss in numbers and bewilderment on the one hand, and a sense of creative ability on the other hand; in fact, a period of crisis.

Industry is outstripping agriculture; and the question which every thoughtful person has on top of his mind—is, "Has rural life had its day; or has it a new day coming; is the farmer a disappearing

*From Address at Tenth National Country Life Conference.

18

human factor in American economics, American social life, American religious life, American politics; or is the farmer about to take a step up in American life, and fill a role,—a fitting new role, which corresponds with the noble pioneer role he has played in the first 200 years of American national life?"

The key to the answer of this question is, in my estimation, the indoctrination of the American farmer and the farm woman in the science of agriculture and the principles of homemaking. Although the first college of agriculture—this college within whose walls we stand— dates back 70 years, although the U. S. Department of Agriculture and the system of Land-Grant Colleges date back 65 years, and although the first state agricultural experiment stations date back 50 years, hope that the American farmer himself would become imbued with the scientific technique of agriculture and household science did not have real evidence in its favor until, less than forty years back, the Hatch Act and Adams Act had got considerable headway, and until after the Smith-Lever Extension Act and Smith-Hughes Vocational Act, had begun to operate with momentum. But beginning with this short period of crisis since 1910, within which is set our special ten-year period, 1917-1927, the principles governing the occupation of farming have come to be the possession of the rank and file of farmers. As Secretary Jardine said in his address at Yale University, March 29, 1927, on Agriculture and Modern Science; "It is no exaggeration to say that through the research accomplishments of recent years the average farmer today knows more of the science on which his industry rests, and brings it into constant application, than the scientists knew fifty years ago."

Lest the significance of the fact that science has become the prevailing factor in farming in America escapes us, let us pause a moment and consider its bearing upon the life side of farming. Let us not as humanists smile this matter off with mild scorn for the reason that this science pertains to the practices of agriculture and not to the practices of human relationships. Indeed I conceive the farmer's scientific attitude of mind with respect to his everyday occupation as but the precursor and herald of the new day in American rural life. Note what this new attitude toward farming means. Is it not a veritable revolution in the mechanique of the farmer's thinking when he substitutes in agriculture a reliance upon accurately observed facts, for tradition, ideas of luck, of irrelevant causation, of fate, of punishment, of vagary, of fear, of superstition? For the rank and file of farmers to be convinced that good things in agriculture follow in a sequence certain ascertainable facts,—which facts may be brought about in the necessary sequence by the farmer himself,—is to have taken one of the most revolutionary steps upward on the ladder of human progress. That this scientific habit of mind pertains as yet almost solely to the practices of agriculture and certain few practices of house-keeping, should not deceive us into thinking that this science is a matter established and isolated in fields and barns and kitchens. No. It is a concept established in the rural human mind; and what is there established as a habit in one department sooner or later becomes operative in all departments of living and its effects may be looked for in due time not only in crops but in human beings.

I am asking you to believe that the great characteristic of rural life in the ten-year period 1917-1927 is the evident revolution in the rural human mind, whereby science has entered as an habitual guide displacing the blind guides. I am asking you to see that science cannot be shut up in a chamber of the mind labeled agriculture, but will pervade all compartments, and sooner or later be in full operation among all the human relationships of rural society. I am asking you to believe that the physiological, psychological, sociological, economic and political aspects of rural society the farmer himself is bound critically to review and reorganize on the basis of the following questions: What are the essential facts now; what in our experience are the invariable sequences of facts preceding good conditions and preceding bad conditions; how shall we go about producing the ante-cedents of good conditions; how shall we go about eliminating the antecendents of bad conditions?

Under this hypothesis of mine, sanitary hogpens and barns are the forerunners of sanitary houses; scientific feeding of cattle, hogs, sheep, and poultry; of wheat plants, corn plants, cotton plants and apple trees, is a mere preface to the scientific feeding of the farm family. Indeed, has not the human come already to share with the hog in the values of protein and vitamin? The pathology of dairy herds paves the way to the social pathology of rural communities. Determined efforts to eradicate the cornborer, are simply indices of the energy which will be expended in eradicating the parasites which at present feed on rural society.

I am asking you to see in the farmer's eager responses to science as applied to the economic aspects of his occupation, a herald of science applied to all his human relationships; and I am asking you as humanists to be happy as you see science capture farming, believing that this revolution in the rural mind will work its way into rural civilization and characterize the second period of the nation's rural life and stand forth as the genius of its culture.

Far be it from me to try to paint a Utopian phantasy with which to soothe your fears in this period of farm population stress. Such a picture would frustrate my objective. I am attempting to see whether there is not hope today for farm people in the ordinary matters of facts. Look about you. Are there not already indigenous examples of the application of a scientific frame of mind to rural human relationships? Note with me in every state the new institutions which are arising in favored communities, where scientific enlightenment has spread rapidly from the compartment of crops to the compartment of people. Count your farmers' hospitals which have arisen in the decade; count your modern rural libraries furnished with book trucks taking books daily to the remoter farm homes; count your modern farm houses, even your modernized farm tenant houses; count up your farmers' modern community club houses, athletic fields, modern swimming pools, count up your consolidated schools, which in the last ten years have insisted on sufficient taxing area to support a school of distinction; count up your farmers' permanent camping grounds, either to county or state; count up your modernized farmers' towns where merchandising has been put upon a scientific basis of service and helpful advertising; count up your rural churches of distinction, the outgrowth of a knowledge of cause and effect. It is not necessary to give here a statistical summary of these almost spontaneous products of enlightenment. The salient facts are common knowledge already. The last ten years have witnessed the spotted upgrowth of these rural institutions in every direction from where you sit tonight. This is the sort of thing which I am asking you to see as the logical outgrowth of agricultural science.

In concluding this sketchy and somewhat dogmatic characterization of rural life in America, what shall we say about the crisis in which rural society finds itself today? During the first two hundred years, cities slowly but constantly gained upon the country and passed it. Cities and industry will doubtless move far ahead of country and agriculture in population. But is the farmer, through continual discouragement and a consequent process of replacement of higher rural intelligence by lower rural intelligence, on the way to becoming a negligible and disappearing factor in American life?

My answer is, no; because the farmers' scientific attitude of mind, and especially his scientific grasp of rural human relationships, is bound to save and is already starting to save rural society for a social role which will be a noble sequel to its social pioneer role during the first 200 years of our history.

PART II. A DECADE OF RURAL PROGRESS

1. HEALTH
   (a) Rural Health and Sanitation, By Walter Brown.
2. HOMES
   (a) The Farm Home, By Grace E. Freysinger.
   (b) The Rural Home, By Mrs. C. A. Steele.
   (c) Rural Electrification, By Frank D. Paine.
3. SCHOOLS
   (a) Rural Education, By Julian E. Butterworth, Katherine M. Cook, Marvin S. Pittman, Verne McGuffey, Helen Hay Heyl.
4. CHURCHES
   (a) The Work of the Major Protestant Bodies, By Malcolm Dana.
   (b) The Catholic Experience, By Edwin V. O'Hara.
   (c) Religion and the Jewish Farmer, By Gabriel Davidson.
   (d) Religion in McHenry County, Illinois, By Carl R. Hutchinson.
5. WELFARE WORK
   (a) Rural Social Work, By Leroy A. Ramsdell.
6. USE OF LEISURE TIME
   (a) Rural Recreation and Social Life, By Harold D. Meyer.
   (b) Communication and Transportation, By T. A. Coleman.
7. GOVERNMENT AND TAXATION
   (a) Rural Government, By E. H. Ryder.
   (b) Tax Legislation, By Charles L. Stewart.
   (c) Benefits from Taxation, By M. H. Hunter.

RURAL HEALTH AND SANITATION*

The Committee on Rural Health and Sanitation found itself confronted with considerable difficulty in assembling sufficient reliable data upon which to base their authoritative report. We lack in America any central health authority whose reports give us an adequate picture of what is happening, particularly in the rural areas. The Committee, however, has been able to secure a large amount of valuable material through the cooperation of various organizations and individuals. It is impossible to acknowledge this help in individual cases and we hope that this statement will be taken as an earnest one of our appreciation.

The Committee has studied with care the reports and activities of the various groups interested in conservation of rural health in an effort to discover the lines of development which seemed to hold the largest significance since the last decade. From these materials have emerged five outstanding activities which are of importance, namely: the control of communicable disease; the improvement of infant and maternal hygiene; the growth of rural public health nursing services; the development of health education; and the increase in hospitals serving rural areas.

County Health Departments

The development of the County Health Unit is the most important advance in rural health service in the history of the American health movement. The county is usually an accepted unit of local government. The County Health Unit had its beginnings in the efforts of the United States Public Health Service to assist Yakima County, Washington, in an emergency due to typhoid fever. The temporary loan of trained personnel to this community demonstrated the effectiveness of trained health workers and led to the establishment of the first full time County Health Unit in 1911. Since that time the Rural Sanitation Office of the United States Public Health Service, under the patient and enthusiastic leadership of Dr. L. L. Lunsden has promoted and assisted in the perfection of this piece of governmental machinery. With the establishment of the Rockefeller Sanitary Commission for

*This report was drafted by Walter Brown, M. D., Chairman Health Committee American Country Life Association.

the contral of hookworm, rural sanitation received increased attention. The re-organization of this Commission and its permanent establishment of the International Health Board gave to rural health workers a new and powerful ally in the development of adequate health service. These two agencies have demonstrated beyond question the soundness of the County Unit and by 1926 we had 307 of these county units.

One significant factor is that they are cooperative enterprises. Two hundred and eighty of them are receiving some financial support from one or more of the following agencies: State Board of Health, United States Public Health Service, The International Board, or the Children's Bureau.

These are encouraging facts but it is still a serious situation when over 84% of our rural population is as yet unprovided with official local health service approaching adequacy. Lunsden has calculated that at the rate of progress since 1920 it will take 85 years for whole time rural health service to be extended to all communities of the United States where it is needed.

The experience of the last decade indicates that the proper foundation for rural health service is the county health unit under the direction of a qualified whole time health officer. By such an agency there can be carried economically and efficiently a well balanced, comprehensive local health service supported by the community through taxation.

Infant and Maternal Hygiene

The passage of the Shepard-Towner Act by the 67th Congress marked a radical departure in the relations of the federal government to state health administration. It was the first nation-wide acknowledgement of the need for better health protection for infants and mothers. This Act made available federal funds to the states for the promotion of infant and maternal hygiene.

The measure was offered as a means of beginning the solution of a long neglected problem. The Children's Bureau of the Department of Labor had for nine years been investigating the maternal and infant mortality in various parts of the country. These investigations had revealed conditions that were startling in their seriousness. Notwithstanding the presentation of facts, it required a most strenuous campaign waged in two congresses before the third (67th) finally agreed to recognize human values as well as property values.

The bill provided for Federal subsidy to every state which accepted the Act. An outright appropriation of $5000 annually; and $950,000 annually to be distributed according to the population of the state appropriated in equal amount. The administration of the Act was vested in the Children's Bureau. The States were given authority to initiate and administer plans subject to the approval of Federal Board of Maternity and Infant Hygiene. The Board is made up of: Chief of the Children's Bureau, Surgeon General, Public Health Service and the Commissioner of Education.

The response to this Act can be estimated by the fact that 42 out of 48 states accepted its provision the first year. Since then all the states except Connecticut, Illinois, Kansas, Maine and Massachusetts are cooperating with the Federal authorities.

During the six years of the operation of this Act the complex problems of carrying the benefits of a maternity and infancy program to all parts of the country have been approached with patience and skill. The policy of the Federal Board has been to consider every plan presented in the spirit of the Act and it has not attempted to control the activities undertaken so long as they were directed toward making America a safer place for mothers and children.

The prospects of the states have had for their objective: (1) Better infant care through the teaching of mothers, (2) Better care for mothers through education to the need and value of skilled supervision during pregnancy, childbirth and the lying-in period, and (3) More widespread medical and nursing facilities.

Notwithstanding the great difficulties involved in such a huge undertaking, it should be classified as a success. It seems strange to a public health worker who knows the dire needs of the rural mother and child that there should be a sufficient number of men in Congress to terminate this Act at the end of two years. For the recent Congress has taken such action. The fine program which has been begun during the last six years will have to stop unless our representatives are given unmistakable evidence that America does value the lives of its mothers and children.

Rural Public Health Nursing

In an effort to secure some idea of the extent and present status of rural public health nursing, the Committee sent letters to the Board of Health in each state, State Tuberculosis Associations, the Department of Public Health Nursing of the American Red Cross, the Research Department of the American Child Health Association and to the National Organization for Public Health Nursing. The returns from these letters were most gratifying. We received replies from all of the National Associations and from 42 states. Thirty-three letters came from the state boards of health and 31 from the state tuberculosis associations. From these replies we are able to present the following facts about the development and present status of this branch of rural health service.

Public health nursing in rural communities had its beginnings before 1917 but its period of most rapid development was between 1918 and 1920. It was stimulated by the war needs and carried over into the peace period. Public health nursing in the rural area is administered under a great variety of plans—official and voluntary. The state tuberculosis associations have been responsible for assisting in the establishment of public health nursing in a large number of states, especially before 1917. The American Red Cross instituted a town and county service in 1911 which was changed to the Public Health Nursing Service in 1913. During the war this organization was very active through its chapters in the various states in stimulating interest and financing rural nursing services. In addition this organization gave scholarships to overseas nurses for public health nursing courses. In 34 of the states the Red Cross is still making some contribution to the salary of rural nurses and in 31 states the tuberculosis association is performing the same service. In many of the states these appropriations supplement those made through public funds. It is interesting to know that there is a state appropriation for rural nursing service in 32 states.

One of the distinct advances has been the legal recognition of the desirability of appropriating public funds for this service. In 40 of the 42 states there is a permissive law permitting an appropriation from county funds for public health nursing. One state has a permissive law which relates only to schools and the school nurse is called a health teacher. In one state, in addition to the permissive law for the county nurse, there is a mandatory law for a public health nurse in the schools. Among the state departments of health, 18 now have a division of nursing. In one state there is an advisory nurse in the administrative division of the health department and in 14 states nursing is combined with child hygiene. Four states reported neither child hygiene nor nursing divisions in the state department of health, while four failed to report on the subject at all. The progress of public health nursing and its present status is of interest. Thirty-eight states reported a steady development in their rural health nursing service. In most of these states there was a distinct slump about 1920 but in many cases this has now been completely overcome. Only four of the states reported a continuation of the slump. It is interesting, therefore, to note that in every part of the country, with the exception of the four states reporting a failure of the public health nursing program to progress, the prospects for the future of public health nursing in the rural communities would seem to be very bright.

There are now 13 states which have courses in their educational institutions for training public health nurses and another states is just establishing such a course. These nursing courses are well distributed throughout the country—in the East, Middle West, and the Pacific Coast. The need at present is not so much the development of more courses in public health nursing but rather the stimulation of the nurses to enter one of the courses already established. A study of the number of students in these courses shows that in most instances they are rather limited.

Hospitals

The extension of hospital service to rural areas has been one of the interesting developments of the last decade. This extension has been brought about by a number of influences among which may be mentioned the diminishing numbers of the country doctor; the mounting costs of city hospital care and the realization of the social and economic advantages of a local hospital.

Previous to 1908 the rural hospital was practically unknown in the modern sense. There were many county homes or poor houses in which a few of the sick poor were given indifferent medical care. The rural hospital movement received its greatest impetus through the enthusiasm and devotion of an Iowa country doctor. He was convinced that if hospitals were good for city people they were of equal value for country people. Further, that it was a community or governmental responsibility to see that this fundamental need was met. The zeal of this individual led him to place the matter before town and county officials; medical societies; and legislators.

The persistent pressing of this problem caused the Legislature of Iowa in 1909 to pass a law providing that the people of counties might tax themselves to erect county public general hospitals. This was the first of such legislation in the United States. The idea has spread. Sixteen states have passed similar laws and others have passed laws according partial powers for securing public funds for hospital service.

The demonstration of this type of rural institution has led in the development of many variations to conform to local needs. The principal types may be specified (1) county hospitals, separate county hospitals and county hospitals connected with county homes; (2) township hospitals; (3) town hospitals; (4) district hospitals; (5) community hospitals; (6) community-private hospitals; (7) southern mountain hospitals. These particular types of hospitals offer such a wide choice of method of establishment and operation that any community can readily find a plan suited to local conditions. Wayne C. Nason has gathered this information in the Farmer's Bulletin No. 1485, United States Department of Agriculture, entitled Rural Hospitals. We are indebted to him for much valuable information.

While commendable progress has been made in this field, much remains to be done before rural America can be adequately supplied with hospital facilities.   Our information about hospitals in the United States has been quite meager previous to 1920.   For five years the Council on Medical Education and Hospitals of the American Medical Association has been systematically compiling information.   The report for 1926 entitled "Hospital Service in the United States" gives a broad view of present conditions.   Unfortunately it has not been possible for them to analyze the rural situation in detail.   The report does show, however, that 1354, or 44%, of our 3069 counties do not have a hospital of any kind within their borders.   This indicates the extent of the rural hospital problem.   At the present time there is one hospital bed for every 141.5 inhabitants in the United States while in the rural areas there is only one bed for 291 persons.

The magnitude of the problem would be discouraging if there had not been signs of real progress during recent years.   The report just quoted shows that since 1920 over 400 counties who previously had no hospital have had one or more built within their borders.

The decision of the Commonwealth Fund to establish a Rural Hospital Program is one of the real signs of recognition of the importance of improved health facilities for rural areas.   After a careful study this organization has embarked upon a plan to assist rural communities in establishing hospital facilities.   They plan to cooperate with selected communities by contributing two-thirds of the capital cost involved in building a hospital in addition to furnishing plans and specifications, advising in selection of equipment and in the organization of the institution for operation.   Farmville, Va., Glasgow, Kentucky, and Farmington, Maine, and two other communities have been able to construct modern hospitals under this arrangement.   The Fund plans to make provision for two such hospitals annually.   This activity marks the first effort to make available for rural America the benefits of the latest developments in hospital construction and operation.

Health Education in Schools

A survey of the literature and activities in the field of health and education indicates that no problem of education is receiving more careful consideration by professional leaders or laymen today than that of the health of school children.   This focusing of attention upon the subject of health is demanding a reorganization of subject-matter and method.   It is placing the proper emphasis upon a controlling factor in the child's education; it is establishing the conception that the period of infancy and childhood is too valuable to be neglected or exploited through ignorance, prejudices or economic gain.

Health education has passed through a series of stages of development, each characterized by the more or less ill-defined and growing conceptions of its function in the school.   In each stage the subject has been named according to the type of knowledge emphasized and the prevailing conception of what knowledge was essential. In recent years the emphasis has been placed upon hygiene, sanitation, physical education, medical inspection, health and nutrition clinics, play and recreation, community and mental hygiene. These titles indicate not only changing conceptions of health; but the breadth and scope of the field and its growing importance to the problem of education.

This change in point of emphasis has not come about by a systematic or scientific study of the problem. It is rather the result of persistent efforts of men and women in the medical, health and educational service; men and women who have seen in the immense wastage of human life, unnecessary illness and death, untold suffering, misery, poverty, and crime; in the widespread influence of superstition, prejudice, and ignorance; and in the apparent toleration of unsanitary conditions: the dire need of a constructive program of health education.

The great number of physical defects found among the children in our rural schools present an appalling situation. That these defects can be prevented and that the problem of health is a problem of education is its hopeful aspect. The solution should challenge the best efforts of American citizens.

Dr. Thos. Wood says: "More than half (about 12,000,000) of the school children in the United States are attending rural schools. Country children attending rural schools are on the average, less healthy and are handicapped by more physical defects than the children of the cities, including all children of the slums."

Such facts portraying the health conditions of the country child and the environment in which he lives are a challenge to any agency interested and responsible for the health and welfare of childhood.

Attempts at the improvement of health education have resulted in a variety of programs, each making vital contributions to the present emphasis and improvement of health. In some localities health education is interpreted as a program of health inspection, with a cataloguing of childrens' defects with little or no follow-up work; in others a scheme of weighing and measuring with a program of intensive drill on specific, fundamental health habits; in other sections open-air schools, milk-feeding stations, with special emphasis upon the problem of malnutrition. Others have placed emphasis upon physical education with a program ranging from prescribed formal exercises to the employment of high-salaried coaches to train a few athletes to play basketball or football, often neglecting the physical activities of those who need it most.

The increasing availability of knowledge of the health conditions of school children in rural schools; the growing interest in the health demonstrations in rural areas; the abundance of health programs and of health materials; the increasing fund of scientific knowledge necessary to helpful living; and the need of well organized curricula in health for rural schools make desirable more studies in measuring the effectiveness of health education.

Health Demonstrations

The growth and popularity of the health demonstration as a method in the health field deserves a separate description, since such a large part of their program is an attempt to meet rural needs.

The first of these Demonstrations was conducted at Framingham, Massachusetts. It was financed by the Metropolitan Life Insurance Company and administered by the National Tuberculosis Association. It aimed to determine how much it would cost to reduce the mortality of tuberculosis to a minimum in a given time. The by-products of community co-ordination were even more valuable than the mere statistical reduction in rates.

The next important development was the establishment of a Child Health Demonstration at Mansfield, Ohio, financed by the American Red Cross and operated by the National Child Health Council. This demonstration was a piece of cooperation with a local community with the objective of finding the ways in which the best procedure in every phase of health could be made available to a local community. Real progress was made in the co-ordination of all the community forces—professional and lay. Through efforts of the Demonstration there was built an intelligent public opinion on health matters which has assured the permanent support and further increase of health facilities to meet the changing needs of the community.

In 1922 the Milbank Memorial and the Commonwealth Funds entered this field. The health demonstration is now being tried out on an intensive and extensive scale backed by sufficient funds and conducted by trained and experienced personnel. The application of the idea is now being made under a great variety of social, political, and economic conditions. These two organizations have approached the problem independently and from somewhat different points of view. While one approaches the health problem by emphasizing tuberculosis, the other emphasizes the health of children from the prenatal period through adolescence. They both are attempting to attain their objectives through the development of a general health program with emphasis on specialized services. Both are working through and with the local governmental agencies. Of the Milbank projects, only one (Cattaraugus County, New York) is in the rural area, while three of the Commonwealth Fund Demonstrations include rural communities (Rutherford County, Tennessee; Clarke County, Georgia; and Marion

County, Oregon). These plans involve the cooperation with official agencies, the voluntary groups and includes in its conception not only disease prevention but also health promotion; and provides for a sufficient budget upon which to operate a complete health service. The theory upon which this method is based is that the American people will adopt more readily what they see in actual operation. It is too early in these programs to estimate how effective they will be. It would be fair to say that the progress made so far is encouraging and that if present reception and beginning local support are any criteria they will make a valuable contribution toward improving rural health and sanitation.

Rural Public Health Associations

One of the outstanding contributions to rural health has been made during the last decade by the rural public health associations. This movement has grown out of the extension of the activities of the National Tuberculosis Association made possible by the extraordinary development of the Christmas Seal Sale.

Originally this national association was interested in the control of tuberculosis. Years of experience taught them that this special disease could not be controlled unless the general health conditions of a community were satisfactory. This led them to a broadening of their objectives to include general health programs.

The form of organization has lent itself admirably to reaching down through the state organization to the smallest units—even in rural areas. These groups of people recruited originally to sell seals are interested in constructive ways of expending the resultant funds to meet local health problems. The financing of public health nurses, nutrition work, school programs and educational activities are all helping to carry the message of good health to rural areas by the simple device of the Christmas Seal.

Personnel Training

The programs for the improvement of rural health cannot hope to succeed without an adequate supply of properly trained personnel. This supply must include physicians, dentists, public health nurses and teachers. It has become increasingly evident during the last ten years that the courses of training for these specialized workers should be based upon a knowledge of needs and conditions of the rural area.

There has been considerable progress during the last few years. Courses in Public Health are now offered at many universities either as part of the medical courses or as special efforts to train health officers. Two large endowed schools have been established at Harvard and Johns Hopkins Universities. There is a great scarcity, however, of any courses where special emphasis is placed upon the preparation for rural service. This gap in our training program presents one of the real problems in the successful promotion of rural health service.

In the field of public health nursing the progress has been more satisfactory. Fourteen states have now provided courses of training. However, many of them also lack any special experience in rural work.

In the field of training teachers in methods of health education there is still a woeful lack of satisfactory courses. With the rapid increase of scientific knowledge there is ample source material. It remains for our normal schools and colleges to convert it into usable materials and secure its functioning in the lives of children through well trained classroom teachers.

One of the interesting developments has been the growth of post-graduate study by the medical group through extension services. These courses have been established in 12 states as a joint project of the State Medical Society and the State University. Through such developments the quality of the medical service is being improved.

The Next Decade

The progress made during the last decade in improving rural health and sanitation is a challenge for the future. From a critical review of this period there emerges several lines along which it would seem most profitable for those interested in rural life to direct their efforts in the present decade.

First and foremost, we should endeavor to secure a truer evaluation of human life. This means that rural leaders in every line must adopt as a basis for their thinking the newer and positive conception of health.

Health is more than a mere absence of sickness. It does mean freedom from disease and defect, but it means more than that. It means a capacity to meet the physical and mental demands and desires with effectiveness and satisfaction. In brief, health means an ability to maintain physiological normals at their highest potency. With this newer conception as an objective, the rural leaders should study the means by which the various health activities can be integrated with the larger plans for rural community life. To the health worker it would seem desirable to give attention to the following points:

1. Further extension of the county or district health unit, with adequate budgets and trained personnel.

2. Improved medical service through increase of rural hospitals and assistance in making the countryside attractive to well-trained physicians.

3. Support for governmental subsidy applied to health, such as Sheppard-Towner Act, to assist sparsely settled communities to share in modern health service.   ,

4. Improvement of physical conditions of the rural school plant and further development of health education in the school program.

5. Stimulation of educational institutions to provide courses of training for rural health workers of all grades. These courses to be based upon rural conditions.

6. Actual co-ordination of all the health services—Federal, State and local. These services to be given their proper evaluation in the development of community organization.

7. Further research—particularly in the field of determining economical, sound methods of delivering to rural peoples their share of the discoveries of scientific medicine.

8. A survey of the factors and conditions of rural life and environment which affect child life and health with a particular study of those limitations which affect the physical, mental, emotional and social aspects of child life.

Walter A. Brown, *Chairman*
John Brown
Fannie W. Dunn
L. L. Lumsden

THE FARM HOME*

The progress made by farm women in the last decade has been aided by rapid development in many fields of service to the farm home. Public funds to the extent of many millions of dollars have been used for this purpose. During this decade public, semi-public and private agencies made contribution to physical, economic, social, religious, recreational and civic well being in the farm home. Their endeavors covered fields of research, organization, manufacture, distribution and a vast service of instruction, interpretation and demonstration. Personal services of many thousands of highly trained and experienced specialists, vast amounts of printed and illustrative matter, and an increasingly efficient rural contact and distribution service have also contributed to present day conditions.

During these ten years many new mechanical services became available for the farm woman. Electric lighting and household machinery, water systems, central heating apparatus, telephones, labor saving household equipment, music reproducing machines, rural free delivery, parcel post, newspapers and magazines, automobiles, radio and good roads became helpful aids to the farm woman and made life easier and richer for her. These numerous services made it possible for the farm woman to make more frequent contacts with neighbors, merchants, educators, and others and to broaden her viewpoint by exchange of ideas, and by increased opportunity for observation, study, and reflection.

Indicative of the many material changes which have occurred in the farm home within the past decade is the following data:

The 1920 government census indicates that at that time 38.7% of all farms reported telephones, 10% of all farms reported water piped into the house and 7% of all farms reported gas or electric light. During 1926 a survey of rural home equipment was initiated by the General Federation of Women's Clubs. This survey was conducted in twenty-eight states and represented 40,697 farms in all parts of the United States. This survey indicated that 57.2% of the farms had telephones; 47.2% reported water at the house; 33.3% had water piped

*This report was drafted by Grace E. Frysinger, United States Department of Agriculture.

into the house; 27.4% reported electricity in the home; 3.2% had gas pipe system in the home. While these are the only data upon which comparable figures are available for this decenimun period, and while these data are not absolutely comparable, it is thought that the changes noted are significant of the change in conditions generally and form an adequate basis for comparison. Other data from this list mentioned study which indicate recent conditions in the farm home are the following:

21% of the homes had stationary bath tubs.
16.6% of the homes had flush toilet.
16.3% of the homes had stationary wash bowl.
33.3% of the homes had stationary kitchen sink.
 8.1% of the homes had furnaces.
34.5% of the homes had kerosene, gasoline or distillate stoves for
86.5% of the homes were screened.   [cooking purposes.
24.4% of the homes had ice refrigerators.
 6.5% of the homes had iceless refrigerators.
17.5% of the homes had vacuum cleaners.
42.3% of the homes had washing machines.
20.3% of the homes had electric irons.
 7.4% of the homes had gas irons.
79.5% of the homes had automobiles.
22.1% of the homes had radios.
35.4% of the homes had phonographs.
37.3% of the homes had pianos.

Still further evidence of this development is the fact that approximately 350,000 farms are not connected with central power lines and that farm owned radios increased from 145,350 in 1923 to 1,252,126 in 1927. This marked advance in the status of farm home equipment is characteristic of changes in every phase of farm home life.

In the field of research, governmental and other public and private agencies have rendered service, and studies in personal and public hygiene, foods and human nutrition, clothing and textiles, household equipment and supplies, the relation of electricity to the farm home, marketing and transportation of farm products, and to a more limited extent research in social well being and in economics of the home, have brought forth new facts of direct importance to the farm home.

By the passage of the national legislation known as the Purnell Act in 1925, additional research in home economics was made possible, a total of 105 research projects in agriculture, home economics and sociology affecting the farm home being reported by 41 states during the fiscal year 1925-26. Various other educational institutions not eligible for Purnell funds have also conducted similar research. In addition many semi-public and privately supported organizations such as educational foundations, commercial concerns and farm organizations are carrying on research directly affecting the farm home. Surveys and studies of a less formal nature have also been carried on by such organizations as State and Federal government departments, rural organizations, General Federation of Women's Clubs, American Library Association, Child Health Organization, Congress of Parents and Teachers, Y. W. C. A., Playground and Recreation Association of America, rural magazines, mail order houses, electrical supply manufacturers, life insurance companies, household supply and equipment manufacturers, and others.

Future progress among farm women necessitates that additional research activities be undertaken. There must be research along economic and social lines as applied to rural home and community conditions. There must be studies of successful farm homes and communities and of the factors which make for such success. Studies must be made of what factors contribute to economic efficiency within the farm home, and each factor enumerated must have detailed consideration.

There must be studies of the management of time and energy, and the management of income. Rural home management research studies recommended by the national committee considering use of Purnell funds include (1) the efficiency of the household plant and the methods of housework; (2) community agencies, such as laundries, creameries and bakeries, as means of reducing the time, energy and money costs of the farm household, (3) the extra-household tasks of the farm women, (4) the economic value of the farm homemaker's work, (5) the consumption habits of farm families in regard to food, clothing, furnishings, recreation and other items from the standpoint of adequacy and economy, (6) the purchasing habits and facilities of farm families, (7) the factors influencing consumption, such as advertising, fashion and price variation, (8) the cash contribution of the farm woman to the family income and (9) family budgeting. Studies are also needed as to the efficiency values of physical well-being and the determining factors in the use of the homemaker's time.

Social researches are also needed. Basic studies having to do with the structure and processes of rural society are needed. In addition studies are needed as to rural spiritual and social satisfactions, family relationships, the cultural and recreational habits and needs of farm people, parental training and child care, and the social effects of economic depression.

Objective studies of the constructive values in rural life must also be given further study by unbiased investigators.

Educational researches are also needed particularly as to desirable teaching methods and procedure for rural adults. Basic principles in educational procedure are similar whatever the environment, but the application of accepted principles of teaching to the particular conditions obtaining in rural areas has only begun to be studied. Rural people are rapidly awakening to their educational needs, and the technical field of educational service must prepare to serve them efficiently.

All research studies of rural conditions must be made by persons with truly open minded, scientific desire for truth. All too frequently in the past, rural studies have been made by urban minded and urban experienced persons unqualified through lack of interest and open-mindedness to undertake such investigations.

After data has been acquired as to rural conditions effort must be made to determine the solutions of such problems as are evidenced. The solution of these problems must be determined not by modifying or adapting such solutions as were found successful when similar problems presented themselves in urban areas, but by endeavor to find solutions entirely adequate for rural conditions.

In addition to further research there is need for more constructive literature as to the worth-while values in rural life. There is need of constructive philosophy of rural life and a philosophers to acclaim it throughout the land.

In all undertakings having to do with rural well being the viewpoint and judgment of rural people must be solicited. Rural men and women may not be so facile in making public utterance of their thoughts but they are generally sound in their judgments and are not limited in their viewpoint by any bounds of precedent or public opinion. In addition rural people are more fully informed as to rural conditions, abilities and limitations.

In all future endeavors, rural women and men must be recognized as independent citizens. They must not be considered wards of the nation nor are they to be considered subservient to nor are they to be patronized by the urban population. Their abilities and achievements must be recognized and applauded and utilized for public benefit. There must be reciprocal recognition of and respect for the special abilities of rural and urban people. There must be exchange of helpful service to the mutual advantage of each until such time as increased density of population makes for similar environment with similar problems and experiences thus eliminating urban and rural consciousness and making for oneness as to quantity, quality and scope of abilities.

Future well being in the nation demands that all persons, organizations, and agencies whatever the field of activity, recognize the

American farm man and woman. The farm woman is increasingly participating in the world of affairs and she is having increasing influence in molding its activities. It were well for the world of the next decade to take cognizance of this fact and plan accordingly.

> Mrs. Vera B. Schuttler, *Chairman*
> Mrs. G. Thomas Powell
> Mrs. Dora Stockman
> Mrs. H. W. Lawrence
> Miss Grace Frysinger
> Miss Anna M. Clark
> Miss Bess M. Rowe
> Mrs. Lola Clark Pearson

THE RURAL HOME*

The rural home maker is confronted with the problem of finding time for the wider contacts of modern life.

Because time is such an important item for the rural home maker the following couplet was taken as a keynote of the section meeting:

Twenty four hours there are in each day,
Eight for work, eight for sleep, eight for play.

An effort was made to analyze the activities of the rural homemaker and make a time allotment for her most important duties as a point of departure for various home makers to make their own applications.

EIGHT FOR WORK

Work was defined as those activities necessary for feeding, clothing and housing the family. Other activities were defined as extra-activities.

Emphasis was laid on the fact that the homemaker, first of all, needs to determine what things are essential for the health and happiness of her family, and to eliminate non-essentials.

Six groups of homemakers should lay particular emphasis on labor savers, short cuts and special aids. These are homemakers with large families, those with small children, with much hired help; those who of necessity must add to the family income by extra activities, ones with invalid or old persons in the family, and those with limited strength.

Those participating agreed that water came first as the mechanical labor saver of most value to the homemaker with electricity second.

Women were urged to analyze their jobs and find out what the large time consumers are in feeding, clothing and housing their families, find out how much time these take and decide whether the time is well spent or whether could be reduced. If the home maker will spend more time analyzing her work and the results she is getting, she will better know whether or not she is "putting first things first."

*Presented at Rural Home Section, Eleventh National Country Life Conference, Mrs. Spencer Ewing, Illinois, Presiding.

Eight for Play

Play was defined as including all activities not included under work.

Keeping fit is the first essential for the homemaker and definite time must be devoted to mental and physical refreshment.

An extra activity of greatest importance to the homemaker is that of creating a physical environment of comfort, simplicity and beauty and speakers stressed the fact that state rather than money was the important factor for either exterior or interior beauty of the home.

One speaker suggested that home makers needed to spend more time on methods for creating an atmosphere including such points as:

The celebration of birthdays
Cultivation of hobbies
Conversation at meal time
Family night, (one night a week at home with
reading or some other family interest provided for.)
The family council

The division suggested for the eight hours of play was two hours for keeping fit, four hours for creating the home atmosphere and two for extra activities such as business, community, religious or social.

In discussing both divisions of the program speakers recognized that each homemaker must make her own adjustments to any plans suggested, but that the thing rural homemakers need first of all is a plan, and the wise selection of activities that go to make a rich and well rounded life.

Some of the speakers appearing on the program were Miss Isabel Bevier, Emeritus professor of Home Economics at Illinois; Mrs. Edith Wager, a Farm Bureau member of Michigan; Miss Clara Brian of the Child Welfare Research Station of Minnesota; Mrs. Jeptha Randolph and Mrs. C. A. Steele, Master Farm Homemakers of Illinois and Ohio.

RURAL ELECTRIFICATION*

Frank D. Paine
Supervisor Iowa Project on Rural Electrification

Electric power is one of the greatest pioneers of the twentieth century.

The rugged pioneers of our father's and forefather's day were farmers first of all. Every day of their existence depended upon the soil. As they pushed out into the wilderness of uncultivated land they spared nothing, not even life itself to make our cities possible.

This is the debt the city owes the farmers. Now as never before, we have the opportunity and facilities with which to repay this debt by giving them a time and labor saver, an ever-ready helping hand, our electric power.

There has never been a time when so much thought has been given to the solution of their problem by economists, agriculturists and engineers. These most competent specialists never lose sight of the fact that cost of production, methods of production and living conditions are most influential factors. They and the farmer recognize, too, the benefits that follow in the wake of electric service. It is natural then that those who are interested in keeping agriculure abreast of the times demand this electric service.

When the needs of the farm and the possibilities of electrifying the farm are considered, there can be no hesitation in saying that the farmer should have electric service, but whether or not this much-desired end can be realized depends in no small measure upon the plan for rendering it being on a sound economic and engineering basis so that the benefits derived will enable the farmer to meet costs and, if possible, make a profit in addition to improving his living conditions.

The engineering and agricultural experiment stations in some twenty-three states came to the conclusion that honest cooperative effort was required for the solution of the problem, and they immediately set about to determine the facts relative to the utilization of electricity on the farm and in the farm home. They have investigated and studied every process used in agricultural production, applying electri-

*From Address at Eleventh National Country Life Conference.

43

city in the form of light, heat or power to each, determining the practicability of it and the cost of operation. Old methods have been improved, new methods have been adopted. Out of these investigations, there has emerged a knowledge of the possibilities of building an electric load on the farm.

Closely associated with these projects is the National Committee on the Relation of Electricity to Agriculture. This is an organization made up of representatives from the American Farm Bureau Federation, the National Grange, the United States Department of Agriculture, the American Home Economics Association, the American Society of Agricultural Engineers, the National Electric Light Association, manufacturers of farm equipment, manufacturers of electrical equipment and others. This Committee has counseled with the projects and served as a central clearing house for the valuable data and information which has been made available.

The results of the three years work have been most gratifying, in fact the accomplishments of the projects have been amazing. The facts and factors concerning the application of electric light, heat and power have been determined. The farm home maker can light the home for twenty-five kilowatt hours per month, do four family washings with two kilowatt hours, iron it with five more. She can furnish an abundant supply of both soft and well water with two or three kilowatt hours. The electric refrigerator, a convenience needed in every farm home, is operated for a month with a consumption of from 50 to 80 kilowatt hours.

The progressive farmer is always interested in applying power to save labor. Results of the experimental work show that he can light his barns and yard with 35 kilowatt hours per month, milk cows a month with 27 kilowatt hours, separate this milk with 2.5 kilowatt hours. These are typical examples of results, complete reports from projects give these facts for over 100 different applications of electricity to agricultural production.

Another most important result which has been obtained is, that farmers, farm organizations, public utilities and manufacturers have not only become keenly interested but have become more optimistic concerning the possibilities of rural service. This interest has stimulated a desire to learn more about the problem; consequently thousands of farmers, a great many farm organizations and others have assembled the available material, studied it, analyzed it and have discovered the actual cost of line construction, the reasons why a rural is different from a urban rate and that from a economic standpoint the consumption per farm should average 1200 kilowatt hours a year. Furthermore, these people conclude that they have a responsibility if electric service is to be provided and they are ready to accept it.

The public utilities have also accepted their responsibility in this matter and have made marked progress in the adoption of policies for the building of rural service lines, the development of a system of rates and the establishment of a rural service department, all of which encourage the promotion of this class of business.

Many power and light companies finance and build the rural service lines, furnishing the transformers, services and meters; thereby, serving the rural customers in the same manner as the city customers. Such a plan relieves the farmer of the investment of $300 to $400, which, oftentimes if required, prevents the customer from purchasing the electrical equipment which he needs to properly utilize the service. Also, the farmer is relieved of the business of operating and maintaining this line, both of which belong to the electric company for they have the organization to handle it. Then, too, proper maintenance is a requisite of satisfactory service.

The usual specification for a rate is that it shall encourage the use of electricity by providing a low rate when the consumption is increased by the use of motors and eletric ranges. One of the most satisfactory rates which has been adopted by many companies in the middle west provides that the customer pay a fixed charge of $3.00 for service requiring a 1½ kv-a. transformer, plus 7c per kilowatt hour for the first 50 kilowatt hours and 3c for all over 50 kilowatt hours. This rate is based on the policy of line extension mentioned above. Electric motors and electric ranges can be used extensively when the kilowatt hours they consume cost only 3 cents as provided in this rate.

With electric service available, the farm home can be made as modern as any city home, the farm can be operated more efficiently and with less labor. It is recognized that farm incomes are limited and that improvements entail cost. Nor should anyone assume financial obligations which cannot be met. However, the progress of the world has been most marked because of the human determination to attain.

We know that there are many problems yet unsolved, the pioneer has many lands yet unconquered, but though progress may be slow yet if each person interested in agriculture will devote some time to the study of this valuable work and the result already accomplished, there will be a greater understanding and more cooperation between the city and rural districts, the producer and consumer.

Gradually as the power lines stretch out from the cities and towns, we are making progress more rapidly and benefiting the farmer—we are paying our debts.

RURAL EDUCATION

Progress during the decade just past has been noteworthy in almost every aspect of rural education. Only relatively few of these aspects and only the outstanding achievements in each can be treated in so brief a report as the one here presented. It is encouraging, however, to record even a few of them, since they represent real progress achieved through difficulties. At the same time, the Committee should sound a warning that we are far from having reached what they believe are realizable objectives in rural education. There is much yet to be done before we can approach a complacent attitude even toward the important and fundamental problem of supplying adequate facilities for a modern type of elementary education to all of our rural children.

For the sake of essential brevity dictated by the limitations to which we are subjected as to the length of this report, it will be presented under the following heads: Progress in Rural School Administration ; Progress in Certificating Teachers through State Laws and Regulations; Progress in Rural School Supervision; Progress in the Training of Rural Teachers; and Curriculum Revision.

A Decade of Progress in Rural School Administration
Section prepared by Julian E. Butterworth, Professor of Rural Education, Cornell University.

Research in rural school administration.—One of the most hopeful signs is the emphasis given in recent years to an intensive study of its many problems. A recent bibliography[1] in rural education covering only the period from January 1, 1920, to September 1, 1926, lists 233 titles, mostly research, under the topics "Administration and Organization" and "Surveys."

Through such studies, the problems peculiar to rural administration are being more exactly defined and new procedures and techniques are being discovered.

Local school units.—Probably our greatest problem in rural school organization has been to secure the development of larger and more effective units of local control.

[1] *Bibliography of Certain Aspects of Rural Education,* Bulletin of the U. S. Bureau of Education, 1927, No. 4.

During the ten-year period we are here considering the changes in regard to township and county control have consisted largely in the granting of increased authority to these larger units. Some states have considered legislation looking toward the county as the local unit, notably Missouri and Indiana. Considerable progress has, however, been made during this time in the consolidation of schools in practically all states regardless of the prevailing type of local unit. The United States Bureau of Education reported 5,349 consolidated schools in 1917-18. Mrs. Katherine M. Cook, after a critical examination of available facts, concluded that there were about 14,000 such schools in 1924 and approximately 15,000 in 1926. From 1918 to 1926 the number of one-room schools decreased, according to the Bureau of Education, from 195,400 to about 160,000. In the East consolidation is moving ahead wtih fair rapidity, but in the Middle West the movement has slowed up, probably due largely to the agricultural depression. For example, Pennsylvania reports 255 consolidations with transportation since 1918, while Iowa reports none since 1923.

A stimulating study of the relative value of one-teacher and consolidated schools was made by a committee appointed by the Department of Rural Education of the National Association.[1] The question was as to how the two types of schools compared in effectiveness of instruction as measured by certain achievement tests. While the consolidated school was found to be superior in this matter, the difference (about one-third of a year's work) was not as large as some consolidation enthusiasts had expected. This has led us to remind ourselves that a larger school in and of itself is probably not superior. Unless we secure through this larger school better teachers, better working conditions, more effective supervision, more complete equipment and the like, most of the reputed advantages of the larger school do not materialize.

Rural administrative thinkers appear to be realizing more clearly that a particular type of local unit is not so important as is the attainment of certain important objectives. Two of the most important are: (1) providing sufficient wealth and pupils for the maintenance of a complete school system; and (2) providing a type of local unit in which the people may be brought to work together for better schools. If these conditions are met we need not be so concerned whether the local unit is a consolidated or community district, a township or a county. Conditions in different States and even in the same States may well justify different types of local units.

Discouragingly slow progress has been made in the county superintendency. In about half the states this office is still an elective one

1 Foote, John M.: *Comparative study of instruction in consolidated and one-teacher schools, Journal of Rural Education, II, 337-351.*

while the salary is often so low that a well qualified person cannot afford to retain the position. In many states the county superintendent is not even so well paid as are some of the village principals over whom he has more or less authority.

State cooperation.—The state department of education has become increasingly conscious, during these recent years, of the problems of rural education and of its own unusual opportunities for leadership in this field. Many state departments have added workers devoting themselves specifically to rural problems. Michigan, 1921, established a separate division of rural education, while New York at about the same time organized a bureau of rural education. While we need to be cautious about developing a cleavage between rural and other education, yet these organizations do recognize that there are educational problems peculiar to the rural field and permit the selection of persons trained to deal with them.

Secondary school facilities.—From 1918 to 1924 the percentage of pupils in high school increased from 7.9 per cent to 14.0 per cent. The rural territory has shared in this increase. States have, in this time, made some further progress toward providing free high school privileges for those living in the smaller districts. The junior high school has begun to receive recognition in the rural territory. Pennsylvania reports that half of her 150 approved junior high schools are in the rural territory.

Finance.—For a quarter of a century states have been recognizing the peculiar financial needs of education in the rural areas. During the decade just passed several of the states have provided special aid for weak districts, agricultural instruction, longer terms, consolidation, and the like. New York has recently provided funds for aiding the less wealthy districts and for encouraging transportation and consolidation. Under certain conditions she pays half the cost of transportation and one-fourth the cost of new building.

While these special forms of aid have been provided as an immediate help, many states have begun to realize that the whole state system of school finance needs reorganizing. Hence proposals have been made that look toward aiding any school, rural or urban, to maintain reasonable standards at a fair tax rate. New Hampshire and New York have in recent years passed legislation that looks toward this system of support. As this principle becomes effective special state aid for rural schools may properly tend to disappear. It is probably safe to say that never has there been such an awareness of the need for equalizing opportunities and burdens and that this has been due largely to the rural financial situation.

Briefly, the writer's judgment is that the last decade may claim progress in these aspects of rural school administration:

1. A long step toward the use of scientific methods in attacking its problems.

2. A marked development in number of consolidated schools with some advancement in the developing of larger administrative control through the county.

3. A recognition of the peculiar problems of rural education and the designation by the state of individuals qualified to deal with them.

4. An extension in the secondary school facilities for children in the rural areas.

5. A greater realization of the special financial needs of rural schools.

6. A tendency toward the humanizing of administration through recognizing more fully its social and psychological aspects.

Progress in Certificating Teachers through State Law and Regulations

Section prepared by Katherine M. Cook, Chief, Division of Rural Education
United States Bureau of Education.

State laws and regulations governing the certification of teachers affect the type of teachers employed in rural communities particularly. Unless the state protects rural children from under-qualified teachers, local school boards, in what they consider the interest of economy, are often satisfied with teachers holding certificates of the lower grades whose services can be secured at a low salary.

Progress in the direction of better certification laws and regulations during the past ten years, particularly those governing the issue of the lowest grade certificates granted to inexperienced teachers, has been marked. A study made in 1911 showed that practically all states were issuing low-grade certificates on examination to which candidates for certificates were admitted without fixed minima in scholarship prerequisites. Entering the teaching profession was a simple matter. Once certificated, a teacher need only seek a position— sometimes through the influence of local friends or relatives, rather than professional qualifications or teaching success. By 1919 a number of states had set up certain scholarship prerequisites both academic and professional, four states having reached the minimum prerequisite of high school graduation and some additional professional training beyond high school of from 6 to 18 weeks for the lowest grade of certificate issued to inexperienced teachers. At the present time 27 states have established a prerequisite of equivalent or higher grade. Nine of the 27 have established one year of professional training beyond high school and four have established two years of professional training beyond high school as the minimum prerequisites for the lowest grade of certificate granted inexperienced teachers. In addition to the 27 states referred to above, six require graduation from a four-year high school as prerequisite to entrance to examination for the lowest grade certificate. Professional courses are usually but not necessarily expected in these states either during the high school course or in addition to it.

In most of the states these achievements have been possible through legislation gradually increasing requirements year by year, setting up a goal of one or two years' professional training beyond high school as a minimum essential for all candidates for certificates to be reached at a stated period, through eliminating the lower grade certificates entirely; and through eliminating the possibility of renewing low-grade certificates so that holders must either secure higher grade certificates or discontinue teaching. Arrangements of the type indicated have enabled states gradually to increase materially qualifications demanded for all certificates, particularly those of lower grades, without creating a teacher shortage and without causing undue hardship to teachers themselves or the institutions which prepare teachers. They have been given ample warning, and time to make such preparation as the revised laws indicated were necessary.

Considerable progress has been made also in the direction of centralizing certificating authority in state officials, usually state departments of education. Certification began as a local function, county and district officials being relatively free to employ such persons as they wished without regard to any but nominal requirements in the matter of certification. In 1911, 15 states had set up state systems of certification; by 1921 the number had increased to 26 states. At the present time, i. e., laws and regulations in force in 1926, 36 states issue certificates and control the whole matter of certificating teachers within their borders. In four additional states the states control certification, county authorities merely issuing certain types of certificates. Centralization of certificating authority in state officials has, therefore, progressed to the extent that 40 states now practice it wholly or to the extent of complete control except a mere formality of "issue" on the part of local officials. Doubtless state centralization will become universal in the United States within the next decade. Centralization of certificating authority has enabled state departments of education and state institutions to raise standards and to promote unity of standards within the state.

Other notable aspects of certification in which progress has been made are toward increased requirements in professional preparation; toward eliminating examination as the sole basis on which certificates are issued; toward a higher degree of specialization, each new special certificate created usually requiring credits in appropriate courses in higher institutions of learning. Among the newer types of certificates are certificates in school administration, in school supervision, special certificates for principals of elementary schools, for secondary schools, for adult classes.

A Decade of Progress in Rural School Supervision

Section prepared by Marvin S. Pittman, Director of Rural Education, State Normal College, Ypsilanti, Michigan.

Possibly no phase of rural education has made more progress than that of rural supervision during the past decade. In 1917 23 of the 48 states employed 37 persons in the departments of education to give special attention to the rural elementary and rural agricultural schools, while today 40 states of the union employ 129 persons in the state departments of education to perform the same charactter of work. While the rural schools were, of course, given some consideration and attention from the very beginning of our school system, it was not until within the past two decades that persons were especially employed by state departments of education and given the particular responsibility of stimulating the improvement of rural schools and as an indication of that special duty given the title of supervisor or inspector or rural or agricultural schools. State rural school inspectors or supervisors were first appointed in the southern states through the benefaction of the General Education Board and other philanthropic funds. So helpful was their work that the states themselves soon realized their value and necessity as is shown by the fact noted above that 40 out of the 48 states now have such supervisors so designated in the roster of the state departments of education.

Rural supervisory service.—The county is the unit for supervision in the majority of states; the superintendent with or without supervisory assistants is the officer in charge.

County supervision of rural schools by employment of supervisors or other assistants for the special purpose of supervising instruction received its inspiration between 1910 and 1915, largely as a result of the work done in Baltimore County, Maryland. By 1920 Maryland, New Jersey, Ohio, Oregon, West Virginia and Wisconsin had made some provision for local county supervision on either a voluntary or compulsory basis. Since that time there has been considerable reorganization and much progress as the following list of states with the number of supervisors they now employ indicate: Alabama 39, Arkansas 2, California 139, Colorado 3, Delaware 7, Florida 12, Idaho 5, Illinois 7, Louisiana 14, Maryland 48 white, 19 colored, Michigan 10, Minnesota 12, Missouri 2, New Jersey 38, North Carolina 29, Ohio 14, Oklahoma 4, Oregon 3, South Dakota 2, Tennessee 6, Texas

22 colored, Utah 18, Virginia 23, West Virginia 71, Wisconsin 108, making a total of 657 persons employed for county service in 25 states devoting themselves exclusively to the business of the improvement of rural elementary instruction.

Training, experience, and salary of supervisors.—Data are not available to show the qualifications and salaries of the supervisors employed in 1917. It may be granted that they were much lower than they are now. A study reported in the *Journal of Rural Education,* May-June issue, 1926, by Anna Schumaker, sets forth the qualifications and salaries of the supervisiors of the 14 states employing the largest number of supervisors. The median age is 25 years, the range is from 22 to 63; the median number of months of training above high school graduation is 28 with a range from 2 to 60 months; 32 per cent of the supervisors hold one or more degrees; the median number of years of teaching and supervisory experience is 14 with a range from 3 to 39; the median salary is $1,800 with a range from $1,000 to $4,000.

A Decade of Progress in Rural Teacher Training

Section prepared by Verne McGuffey, Teachers College,
Columbia University.

Among the factors influencing the training of teachers are the certification standards set by the state and the salaries paid by the local communities. Improvements in these factors go together. The advancement in training of rural teachers during the past decade is due largely to more rigid certification laws and a marked advance in salaries.

Teacher preparation on the secondary level is decreasing in importance. Some states have abandoned the training in high schools entirely and others have added a fifth year to the course. Training teachers in high schools is at best a temporary expedient and should be recognized as such. As soon as possible the burden for training all teachers should be placed on the normal school and teachers colleges where it belongs.

Ten years ago four per cent of rural teachers had an academic preparation less than that represented by graduation from the eighth grade and only 45 per cent were graduates of a four-year high school course. At that time one-third of the rural teachers had no professional training and less than five per cent were normal school graduates.

The period from 1917 to 1927 has shown an improved and widespread realization on the part of teacher training authorities of their duty towards the rural schools. During the three-year period from 1915 to 1918 the number of departments of rural education in such institutions practically doubled. The agricultural depression following 1920 checked the advance, and in some states there was an actual loss, but the past three years have seen considerable progress in all phases of rural teacher training.

A study made by Verne McGuffey and R. L. Bunting under the direction of Professor Mabel Carney, during the spring of 1927, shows the present status of rural teacher training so far as state normal schools and teachers colleges are concerned. The study is based on reports from 149 institutions. Of these, 60 report a distinct group of students preparing for rural teaching. Ninety-five of the institutions reporting offer a two-year course for prospective rural teachers, 53 offer a one-year course, 21 offer a three-year course, and 46 a four-year course. More than one curriculum for rural teachers is offered by 69 institutions. Nine of the institutions report that they plan to enlarge their rural work next year. One hundred three institutions report one or more members of their faculty giving their time to rural education.

The returns from the above study show that 54 institutions have a total of 350 one and two-room schools used for practice teaching in training student teachers. Forty-one institutions report the use of 80 consolidated and village schools for practice purposes. A total of 85 institutions report provision for observation and practice teaching in rural schools.

Fifty of the institutions reporting show that 4,710 persons *graduating* from their rural courses last year are now teaching in rural schools. Seventy-two institutions report a total of 11,627 of their last year's *students* now teaching in rural schools. An average therefore of 162 from each of the 72 institutions. Several institutions report that practically all of their graduates go into rural schools, including, of course, the small towns and villages as rural. This is in contrast to data collected about 1915 showing only about ten per cent of the graduates of normal schools going to the rural communities. It is of interest to note that the study referred to shows 91 institutions carrying on some form of extension service.

It is worthy to note that of the normal school graduates who do go to the rural schools that less than half have had any particular training for the peculiar problems which they must meet. Normal schools and teachers colleges are not meeting their responsibilities in this respect.

Compared with a similar investigation made by Professor Mabel Carney in 1924, the study referred to shows some expansion of rural activities in normal schools and teachers colleges but that even yet only a few are meeting in any adequate way the problem of training teachers for the rural schools. Every school charged with training prospective rural teachers should have an adequate faculty of rural specialists and provide a differentiated curriculum of studies and facilities for practice teaching in rural schools for all those who expect to teach in rural communities.

One of the difficulties in training rural teachers is to secure an appreciation of rural life and its problems. The report shows 45 institutions have a rural club with memberships ranging from 14 to more than 300. Membership in such a club as an integral part of the training for rural teaching develops such an appreciation.

The length of training for positions in the rural field should be as long as for corresponding positions in the cities. The solution of the problem of enrolling in rural departments a sufficient number of prospective teachers and retaining trained teachers in rural schools apparently presupposes standard qualifications and salaries as high as those paid teachers in urban communities.

Revision of the Rural School Curriculum

Section prepared by Helen Hay Heyl, Assistant in Rural Education, The University of the State of New York, The State Department of Education, Albany.

Some present characteristics and objectives of the rural school curriculum.—In general, the present tendency in the new rural school curriculum is to offer an education to country boys and girls along broadly cultural lines. The school is to be conceived of as a social group where children learn the art of social living.

Its purpose is to so lead the rural child by means of a broad outline of studies into his peculiar social inheritance that he can take pride in being a farm child, and at the same time come into a deepened knowledge of his partnership with the nation and an understanding of his ability to take his place in any phase of American life to which his native capacities and acquired interests may lead him. In brief, the aim of this new rural course of study is:

(1) To develop personality in every child that the school touches.

(2) To develop in this rural child an increasing sense of social responsibility. This implies not only making the child a better individual—healthier, happier, more efficient; but it implies also leading him to become increasingly eager to improve the society of which he is a part.

The modern rural curriculum must harmonize preparation for future living and improvement of the child's present life. It must seek to improve the child and to help him improve his own social child-group through the gradual development of social responsibility.

(3) The third aim of the new rural school curriculum is to help the country child start on the road toward "self-education." The real test of any school is how the child grows (learns) when he is not a part of it. The real test of any teacher is that she leaves the child

with a desire to know more. The real test of any curriculum is that it arouses the child to continuous educational activity, that it makes him an investigator, an initiator, a permanent—not a temporary student.

Cited in more familiar and succinct terms, the major objectives of the curriculum from children on each level of educational attainment are as follows:

I. *For the elementary school period* (ages 6-12).—(1) Health efficiency, (2) command of fundamental processes [reading, writing, arithmetic, etc.,], (3) worthy home-membership, (4) civic education, (5) worthy use of leisure, (6) ethical character, (7) and in connection with these, the gradual acquiring of vocational information that later may be used by the children as a basis for vocational choices.[1]

II. *On the next level, the junior high school period of education* (ages 12-15), all of the above objectives still function, except the last. This now develops into definite vocational guidance, based on the vocational information which is still being acquired. This period is the "trying-out," the exploratory phase of life, and pupils, especially in rural schools, should have a curriculum which will provide opportunity for the rural child to know about many occupations and professions. This is especially needed for the country boy in that life about him places great emphasis upon one type of work, *agriculture*. That there should be no attempt to encourage any group of children to enter a particular occupation by undue emphasis upon it during the elementary and junior high school ages, or even during the senior high school period where the door should still swing wide to many life opportunities "is one of the distinctive and outstanding characteristics of American education and is deemed essential to democracy." [2] For without this emphasis upon "equality of opportunity," without this privilege of free choice in one's life work, caste lines would be rapidly drawn and a rural peasantry would soon develop in America.

III. *On the senior high school level*, however, there is a distinct place for vocational, or at least pre-vocational training, and so the objective of *vocational education* can be properly added to those listed above on this level. But such vocational education should be freely chosen by pupils and should in no degree rest upon "indoctrination."

With these objectives clearly in mind, it becomes easier to examine the differentiation that must exist between rural and urban curricula. The principal difference which is recognized today is the difference of

[1]*Cardinal Principles of Secondary Education*, United States Bureau of Education, Bulletin, 1918, No. 35, for points 1, 2, 3, 4, 5, 6—point 7 is a supplementation.

[2]Professor Mabel Carey, in Objectives in Public School Education (American) Form 338. Mimeographed matter, Teachers College.

environment. The rural child's farm life experiences form the apperceptive basis for his daily education, and it is necessary to use such skills, knowledge, and attainments as he already has to lead him into a mastery of his environment—for this must be a part of his true education. Certainly in three respects this environment forms part of the rural curriculum: (1) It offers the approach to the subject studied; (2) It provides the resources, the materials for these studies; (3) It indicates where supplementations must be made. The rural curriculum, therefore, uses the rural environment, the "local setting," as a means of approach to the subjects of the curriculum; as a basis for selecting, adapting, and interpreting rural resources in light of the educational activities within the school group; and as a means of discovering and understanding the "lacks" and "needs" of the rural child. It is thus the country child may come to have widened interests, may discover new activities, may grow into an understanding of living conditions, problems, and interests of people in the world at large.

In effect, the rural school and its curriculum has a work to do much like that of the farmer. It must promote growth and development in the child as the farmer does in his crops—by making the conditions right under which the fullest and best fruitage of life may spring into being. "Education can not produce life; but it can produce the conditions under which life may grow."[1]

Conclusion.—But rural education can not, at the present time, serve the rural child through the school alone, for rural schools have not yet regained sufficient strength for the complete and enlarged task of modern education in spite of the immense strides which have been made in the past ten years. The new rural curriculum will demand for some time to come the best thought of every rural agency taxed with the obligation and offered the opportunity of doing rural educational work. And if this new curriculum is to be administered by joint enterprise, then the greatest need of the present is for coordination and affiliation of the educational purposes of the various groups attempting to help the country child. As a first step, this concluding suggestion is made: First, let all rural agencies, working either through the rural schools or *for children of school age* carefully study the curriculum objectives for each level of childhood and youth, and bring their own educational objectives for each level, or age-group, into proper agreement. Second, these agencies—health, recreational, social, religious, economic, including the group which is called "The School"—should build a common curriculum, which directed at present by these now accepted aims, and working under the cooperating supervision of the purely educational group, will serve a larger number of rural children in a better and more forceful way, and will in large measure blot out

[1]Hart's "Light from the North."

supposed differences in feelings, opinions, and purposes, while preventing the "under-looking" and over-lapping" in the rural "job" now so common. To do this rural workers everywhere must

"Put the game above the prize
And hold the cause above renown,"

for only thus can the rural curriculum become truly effective and rural youth be truly served.

Katherine M. Cook, *Chairman*
J. E. Butterworth
M. S. Pittman
Verne McGuffey

THE WORK OF THE MAJOR PROTESTANT BODIES

By Malcolm Dana

Director, Town and Country Department, Congregational Church, Extension Board.

I have been reviewing in my own mind some of the changes, shifts and trends which it seems to me have been increasingly apparent over the country. These seem to manifest themselves in spots, as it were, rather than well defined or mass movements everywhere to be seen. Different sections of the country manifest the same trends for different reasons, e. g., the coming together of churches comes in the east quite largely from economic pressure where elsewhere it is clearly because of a genuine change of religious interest and conviction. One is pessimistic here and optimistic there. On the whole, however, he is blind indeed who cannot see progress in right directions. Patience is needed to realize that a decade is after all a very small area of time in which to make observations.

In the last ten years here are some of the trends I have observed over the country at large, and, as I have said, manifest in no general movement but in spots. The latter are the leaven which will increasingly leaven the whole lump of achievement.

A. I list a few of the trends observable of *negative* character.

    a. The open country church seems to be disappearing, and people are not coming in to centers as they should for religious privilege.

    b. There is a distinct loss of church interest; and denominational specialties and symbolic features—baptism, communion, liturgies—are losing force.

    c. There is a deplorable lack of home religious training and a general turning over of such things to strangers.

    d. There is an increased refusal of young folks to accept the religion of their parents just because it was theirs—and a disinclination to church-going.

    e. At a time when such things are officially deprecated and disavowed by the various denominations there is a persistence of religious competition and over-churching.

    f.   There is as yet no large appreciation of the need for promotion of technic and efficiency in the rural minister and country church comparable with that prevailing in machine farming and scientific agriculture, nor is the farmer's minister given the helps that the farmer can get (right where he is) from a dozen free sources merely for the asking.

    g.   State officials, and rural ministers themselves, are not giving summer schools, and the like, held at agricultural colleges any larger patronage and support.

    h.   It is a question whether personal religiousness, as such, and as formerly powerful, is not decadent.

B.   Opposed to these negative manifestations, which in many ways discourage, are, it seems to me, *positive* trends more than offsetting them.

    a.   The consolidated school is prophetic of a "consolidated church" which is already here—centering in towns and villages and supplemented by an extension equipment and service. The "Larger Parish," both the name and the ser-service "over areas as well as churches" is increasingly practiced.

    b.   There is an increased consciousness of "rurban" common interests on the part of town and village dwellers and peoples of the open country; the former accepting the trade-zone as "community" and the church accepting it as "parish."

    c.   There is increased charity and cooperation between churches and denominations; and a steady growth of the independent "Community Church" and the federated church. Communities are being increasingly allowed to decide just how much religious privilege they want and can pay for, and of what kind.

    d.   There is an increased trend toward the sociological appreciation of religion with "socialization" seen to be the main duty of rural minister, church and religion.

    e.   There is an increased emphasis upon religious education on the part of all religious forces, and Daily Vacation Bible Schools, Week-Day Schools of Religion—with multiplying and more and more efficient equipment and courses obtainable are springing up on every side. Young People's Conferences, with increased emphasis upon genuine discussion and an issue of "doing things"—are taking the place of emotional and talky-talky types of young folk's organization.

f.   There is increased thinking among young people, their own thinking, and a spoken desire for "the Jesus Way" and "dynamics of Jesus" which shall be manifested in social and Christian service.

g.   There is an increased sense of guilt on the part of church officials and "over-head" in matters of religious competition and wasteful duplication of effort.   Talking is showing signs of *doing* righteously.   Such organizations as the Federal Churches of Christ in America, the Home Missions Council, the Council of Women for Home Missions are quietly absorbing the different faiths and orders.   The Lauzanne conference at Geneva is now on and what is said there may result in something *done* at a Church Comity Conference being set up by a joint committee of the above organizations next January.

h.   There is a steady, though discouragingly small patronage of the summer schools for rural workers held at seven agricultural colleges the country over.   These are accredited and present a three year approved curriculum.   Religion is increasingly getting an agricultural approach as emphasized by such organizations as the American Country Life Association, International Agricultural Missions, etc.   The literature bearing on the country church and its work is so over-abundant as to need wise discrimination as to what is worth while.

i.   There is an increase amongst the denominations and churches in the employment of full time, paid rural secretaries and the establishments of Town and Country Departments.   The Town and Country Committee, consisting of all Protestant secretaries of this kind, is doing some very significant things.   The Institute of Social and Religious Research is one of the truly great contributing agencies in the whole field.

j.   While there may *seem* to be a decadence in "personal religion," that is an open question!   For, in contradiction, there is a sure increase of interest in an ethical and social religion with an increasing disinterest in institutional religion.

C.   I have been asked to "prophesy" for the next ten years.   That is dangerous work.   I might beg the question by maintaining that the above *positive* trends are likely to increase in momentum and universality everywhere.   They will, to my mind, with modification and adaptation, where the future shall show its need.

In a general way, the following seems to me likely to continue throughout coming years. I adapt these points from an address I gave at the National Council—the highest assemblage of my own denomination—at Omaha last May.

The following are a few of the shifts and changes going on around us with certain implications:

    a. Decreasing and changing populations upon the soil are obliging folks of different nationalities, creeds and temperaments to learn how to live and work together. This increased mingling of these peoples in their social, political and farm organizations, is stimulating a growing desire for the like practice of democracy in religion. Larger and more inclusive church groups must be the order; groups which will fellowship with and look after all.

    b. Aloofness and individualism have been the farmer's bane. He is discovering now-a-days the fallacy of the familiar dictum that "competition is the life of trade" and he knows that it cannot be the life of farming. So he is pooling interests to get together what he cannot get singly; and farmer "cooperatives" are setting both example and pace for the country church. The farmer increasingly wants a practice of religion which will be a unifying and not (as it has been) a decisive force throughout the "rurban" community.

    c. The "little red school house" is almost gone and the consolidated school is giving to country youth an abler teaching, better equipment and larger associational fellowship. The taxable unit becomes more akin to that of the cities. Even so, this consolidated school is prophetic of something akin to a "consolidated church" which will not neglect the open country but increasingly serve it by recognizing, with the country merchant, that the trade-zone is the community and must therefore be the "parish." The consolidated church, as it is the pooling of interests of the many rather than the few, can get and hold a competent ministry; the latter being a multiple one with a departmentized division of labor and an efficient extension equipment and service. Villages and towns are service stations for the open country (or should be); this central church will be.

    d. An abnormal "escape from the country" is convincing folks of the countryside that the very "bright light" institutions which are drawing their young people especially, away from the farms, must be brought—in adapted ways and forms—to the country. The church has always been looked to as central by country people. They are looking to it now to do this thing—by some wise plan of selection and supervision. Salvation is being sensed as social, economic, and even recreational, and the conviction increasingly obtains that men themselves, and their environments, must be saved as well as their souls. All this calls for a new type of minister but gives lure and challenge to the rural ministry. A religio-social program is wanted, and the rural minister need not be one whit less a man of God because he can also be a community builder, a rural life engineer and a local statesman."

THE CATHOLIC EXPERIENCE

By Edwin V. O'Hara

National Catholic Welfare Conference.

1. The good roads era and auto transportation have vastly improved regular attendance of Catholics living in the country at church services. For the most part Catholic churches are situated in the towns, so few churches have been adversely affected by the improved transportation.

2. The strong Catholic Parish schools in towns and cities have led many Catholic families to move to the larger centers to give the children religious education.

3. The Rural Life Bureau of the National Catholic Welfare Conference, and the Catholic Rural Life Conference—organized by the Bureau, have created a larger interest among Catholics in country problems, and are improving the methods of country parish administration.

RELIGION AND THE JEWISH FARMER

By Gabriel Davidson,
General Manager, Jewish Agricultural Society.

If religion forms a problem in the life of all farmers, that problem is intensified in the case of the Jewish group. Christian farmers have their churches and their religious organizations handed down to them as a legacy from former generations. The Jewish farming communities are young and, therefore, the present day Jewish farmers have no such heritage. They must build for themselves, no easy task for a pioneer generation. For two thousand years the Jew has been ready to sacrifice all for his faith, and now in the land of religious freedom, he is not prepared to surrender his ancient ideals. The problem is a difficult one and, yet, much progress has been made within the last ten years.

Despite the fact that the main effort of The Jewish Agricultural Society is directed toward building up the farmer economically, it has never lost sight of his spiritual needs. Through outright contributions and by means of loans repayable over long periods and without interest, it has aided the construction of synagogues and religious centers in farming communities throughout the country. It has not been able to subsidize religious education but it has enlisted the cooperation of the United Synagogue of America, an association interested in communal religious work, and has obtained subsidies from the synagogue toward the maintenance of a number of schools in Connecticut, New York, New Jersey, Pennsylvania and Michigan. It is hoped that this work will be extended.

The difficulty of providing religious education for farm children lies in the fact that even in comparatively compact communities, distances between farm homes are big. It is hard to get together a sufficiently large group to pay for the services of a teacher even where the parents are relatively well to do. Our plan calls for the pooling of the resources of two or three communities close enough for an instructor to travel from one to another, and yet too far apart to assemble the children in the same school. In this way each group can receive instruction two or three times weekly. This plan reduces the cost to each community. Each group of schools is governed by a board of education composed of members selected by the farmers and representatives of the United Synagogue and of our Society.   These school boards appoint the teachers and have charge of general school matters. The Synagogue advises on questions pertaining to curriculum, and our Society on subjects of fiscal policy.   Teachers are selected not only from the point of view of their pedagogical qualifications but of their ability to develop into Jewish communal leaders.

Sabbath schools are also organized by the Department of Farm and Rural Work of the National Council of Jewish Women.   That Department likewise carries on a correspondence course for children, who, because of distance, cannot attend any school.   The Young Israel, a monthly publication issued by the Union of American Hebrew Congregations, is distributed in Jewish farm homes.

Jewish farm communities are growing in size and influence.   With this growth they are becoming ever more alive to their religious needs; likewise, better able to meet them.   If I were to make a forecast for the next decade, I would simply say that the work for which the foundation has been laid will be considerably strengthened and that material progress will be accompanied by even greater spiritual advance.

RELIGION IN McHENRY COUNTY, ILLINOIS*

CARL R. HUTCHINSON
Research Associate of Arthur E. Holt, Chicago Theological Seminary

A Study of Two Hundred Farmers

PURPOSE OF STUDY: To discover relationship between the church and the farmers in the dairy district of the northwest of Chicago.

An attempt was made to discover the relation between church membership and the membership in progressive farm organizations and in other ways to evaluate the place of religion in the farmer's life. The Survey was especially interested in the farmers who tested their cows before the city forced them to do so. Here was a group who acted from motives other than legal compulsion. How were they motivated? A general average was established as a basis of comparison.

Our study of the dairy farmers of McHenry County began April 1, 1926, the day the Chicago Ordinance against milk from untested cattle went into effect. Fifty farmers in Richmond Township were visited and findings were fully written up.

Starting with the insight which came out of this intensive study a tentative schedule was prepared for the purpose of making a more comprehensive study of the Dairy Farmer.

This schedule which included 100 questions was tried out on 25 farmers chosen from different parts of the country. The questions were then carefully examined for ambiguity and duplication.

It was found that in order to answer some of the main questions which we wanted answered about the dairy farmer a more elaborate schedule was needed. This was built out of the trial schedule, and is the one used in gathering the material which is the basis for the following report of findings.

In order to get a representative sample of the dairy farmers of McHenry County, it was finally agreed that:

(a) The selection must not be left to the whim of the worker.

(b) That the farmer must not be selected because of openness to approach.

Presented at Rural Church Section, Eleventh National Country Life Conference.

(c)   Nor because of geographical accessibility.

(d)   And that cases must be taken at fairly regular geographical intervals. To meet these demands this principal of selection was hit upon: taking every alternate intersection of section lines, those two farmers were to be interviewed who lived nearest these points. In case one or both of these farmers were not accessible, the next closest was chosen.

The worker secured the 200 cases out of 210 attempts.

Each farmer was interviewed at his home. Most of the interviews took place in the house. Others occurred in the barn or field. The average time required for each case was about one hour.

The county veterinarian's records show a total of 2,216 dairy herds in the county. Our 200 cases then represent nearly 10% of the total dairy farmers. We feel that this is a fairly representative sample, when it is recalled that the principle of selection was objective and we believe sound; and that it was strictly adhered to in the survey.

The Dairy Farmer and the Church

What are the church preferences of these 200 farmers?

    50 Catholics
    66 Lutherans
    35 Methodists
    12 Baptists
     8 Congregationalists
     1 Universalist
    20 (No preference)
    ——
Total 200

What percent of these are church members?

    86% of those indicating Catholic preference
    76% of those indicating Lutheran preference
    75% of those indicating Congregational preference
    43% of those indicating Methodist preference

What proportion of farmers have radio connection with church?

    53% of the 200 farmers listen to church radio services.
    70 farmers prefer "The Little Brown Church" or services from Moosehart, Indiana.
    36 prefer Zion City
    34 prefer Paul Rader or Moody Church
    10 prefer University of Chicago or Sunday Evening Club

What do farmers think of the church?

    34.0% graded as "strong" for the church

    22.5% were moderate for the church

    36.0% were weak in their endorsement for the church

    7.0% were neutral

    0.5% were opposed to the church

What Are Major Obstacles to Regularity of Church Attendance?

CHORES: The average time required to do the Sunday morning chores is three hours and fifteen minutes. Farmers as a rule attend church at the expense of more effort than village people. Sunday becomes their busiest day.

DISTANCE: Under average conditions it requires the average farmer sixteen minutes to drive to church after he has finished his work at home.

CHILDREN: Twenty three per cent of these farmers have children under three years of age.

Unusual happenings and hazards connected with the care of farm animals keep many farmers at home.

Is the Village Church Making an Attempt to Reach the Farmer?

51.0% of all farmers received no calls from minister during year

34.0% of all farmers received 1—2 calls

11.5% of all farmers received 3—5 calls

3.5% of all farmers received 6 to more calls

Of the church members—

43% received no call from minister

33% received 1—2 calls

15% received 3—5 calls

4% received 6 or more calls

Why do Dairy Farmers Support the Church?

Many farmers gave more than one reason.

88 farmers felt it their duty.

86 felt a need of the church.

68 believe it necessary to their soul's salvation.

15 believe they should set an example to others.

6 go to church for fellowship.

What Reasons Do Farmers Give for Not Supporting Church?

Many farmers gave more than one reason.

51 say they are too busy.

10 say they do not feel the need.

5 say they do not like certain members.

4 say the do not like the minister.

4 say they do not feel welcome.

48 gave other reasons.

What Relation Between Church Membership and Membership in Progressive Social Organizations?

Two thirds of these who are strong for the church are strong for Farm Bureau and Pure Milk Association.

Whereas those who are strong for the church represent only one-third of total farmers yet this group furnishes two thirds of those who rate strong for constructive farm organizations.

22% of those indicating no church preference belong to Farm Bureau or Pure Milk Association.

22% of the Catholics belong to Farm Bureau or Pure Milk Association.

32% of the Lutherans belong to these organizations.

35% of the Methodists and Congregational belong to these organizations.

What is Relationship Between Church Membership and Responsiveness to Idealistic Motives?

Although those who are strong for the church represent only one third of total farmers yet this group furnishes 42% of those who tested early.

Of this 42% who tested early 85% of these gave humanistic motives for testing.

General Summary

Dairy Farmers as a class are not opposed to religion or the church.

There are natural obstacles to regular attendance which do not exist for the village man.

The ministers have called on less than half of these farmers during the past year. 43 per cent of the church members had no call from a minister during the past year.

People who join churches also join the Farm Bureau and the Pure Milk Association in larger numbers than those who do not.

People who joined churches furnished a high percentage of those who tested early before the city forced them to do so.

In an increasing number the farmers are turning to the radio for religious services.   Paul Rader and the Moody Church get three and one half times the hearing that the University of Chicago and Sunday Evening Club receive.

27% farmers approve the action of the city in demanding T. B. free milk.

27.5% farmers approve the T. B. Program of the State and Federal Government.

Those who avoided the crisis by testing early are found in these groups.

78% of those who rate very strong for the church are in these groups.   They were prepared.

Is it the function of the church to prepare folks for crises by making them alert and by bringing them to an honest facing of the situation?

RURAL SOCIAL WORK*

This report deals only with the central, well-defined field of social work, comprising (a) care for broken or incapable families requiring outside help; (b) care for abused, neglected, dependent, delinquent and otherwise handicapped children, requiring care, protection, or supervision by others than their parents; (c) care for the aged dependent; (d) care for or supervision of feeble-minded and metnally diseased persons; (e) treatment of criminals. As the last two classes are commonly handled by state institutions they are relatively less important in the present discussion than the others. The above fields of activity do not constitute the entire field claimed by the social work profession. Recreation and public health education, for instances, are considered by social work to be within its field. Those various "border-fields" of social work are excluded from this report on the assumption that they will be covered by other committees of the Association.

PART I. DEVELOPMENTS IN LAST TEN YEARS

I. METHODOLOGY.

    A. In the central field of social work.

        1. Recognition of the necessity for modifying city-bred methods and ideas to suit rural conditions has become increasingly evident in the discussions of rural social workers.

        2. The concepts of the general social case worker and of the general social worker have definitely emerged and won serious consideration.

        3. Rural social workers have shown an increasing tendency ignore the various specializations within the field of social work.

11. ORGANIZATION AND ADMINISTRATION.

    A. In the central field of social work.

        1. The county has become firmly established as the normal unit for local administration in this field.

*This report was drafted by Leroy A. Ramsdell, New York School of Social Work, Chairman.

70

2. Probably eight hundred rural counties have been organized for service, employing at least one full time social worker.

3. At least three states have established bureaus,—usually called bureaus of county organizations,—within their respective departments of public welfare for the promotion and improvement of local administration of social work chiefly in rural territory.

4. Several state councils of social agencies have been established but none seem to have achieved genuine success.

5. The National Council of Agencies engaged in Rural Social Work has been organized and has led to some interesting experimentation by some of its constituent agencies in the coordination of work.

6. At least three distinct and successful approaches to the development of rural social work have been well worked out during this period.

   a. The method of promotion, county by county, by a state wide private agency, best exemplified by the thirty years' activity of the Division of County Organization of the New York State Charities Aid Association.

   b. Promotion in a similar manner by public state agencies without special legislation exemplified by the work of the University of Iowa.

   c. The method of statutory creation of county social agencies, under the supervision of a state department, as has been done in North Carolina and Minnesota.

7. In at least nineteen states there is now some state wide agency, public or private, which is definitely concerning itself with the promotion of social work in rural areas.

8. Several different methods of setting up social services in the rural county have been tried out successfully—for instance—

   a. A purely private county organization with a definite service program employing a social worker from funds raised by voluntary subscription, such as the Red Cross.

   b. A private organization contracting with the county authorities and using both public and private money in employing a social worker. The State Charities Aid County Committees in New York are examples of this type.

    c. A purely public agency with a definite and limited service program employing one or more social workers, —for example, the Child Welfare Boards in Minnesota, and the Mothers' Allowance Boards in Pennsylvania.

    d. A purely public agency with a broad and inclusive welfare program like the County Boards of Public Welfare in North Carolina.

    e. A federation including both public and private agencies and having a broad and inclusive welfare program. Examples are the County Welfare Federations in Florida, and the County Social Service Leagues in Iowa.

9. Other interesting approaches to the development of rural social work which have not yet proved themselves to be generally applicable are the following:

    a. The employment of visiting teachers by county school authorities. Several demonstrations of this kind have been made under the auspices of the Commonwealth Fund.

    b. The employment of social workers by cooperative societies which was tried by four large cooperative marketing associations among farmers.

    c. The extension of the services of city social agencies to the surrounding rural territory.

III. RESEARCH.

Of genuine research bearing directly upon rural social work, there has been very little, and that has dealt for the most part with the demonstration of a need for rural social work and with methods of organization and administration in this field. Much of the research in rural sociology has had some value for rural social work, but not to the degree that might be desired. The following summary of research developments in this field is exceedingly sketchy and incomplete.

1. Slightly antedating this ten year period was the study of rural juvenile delinquency in New York made by Kate Holladay Claghorn for the Federal Children's Bureau.

2. Perhaps the most noteworthy of the subsequent studies of the Children's Bureau in this field was that of County Organization for Child Care and Protection, published in 1922.

3. During this period the National Child Labor Committee has made a number of studies in the rural field. Notable among these are the studies of child labor in the beet fields, the cranberry bogs, and other specialized agricultural environments, and the study of child welfare in West Virginia which was published under the title of *Rural Child Welfare.* (Macmillan)

4. A great deal of research for local purposes, has been carried on in some states by public or private state agencies.

IV. TRAINING OF RURAL SOCIAL WORKERS.

1. At least ten schools in the Association of Training Schools for Social Work have added courses in rural sociology or rural social work to their curricula during this decade.

2. Two of these training schools, those at the University of North Carolina and the University of Missouri, have set up more or less complete programs of training aimed definitely at the preparation of social workers for the rural field.

3. More recently some of the state and national agencies have begun experimenting with the training of workers for the rural field in some of their county units. In some cases these experiments in apprentice training have been combined with theoretical training at schools of social work.

4. The institutions which several of the state conferences of social work have begun to develop are not without significance in this connection, since many of the workers who participate in these "short courses" are public officials and social workers from small towns and rural communities.

V. DISCUSSION AND WRITING.

1. More than half the state conferences of social work have reflected the increasing interest in the rural field in their programs.

2. At least half a dozen such conferences have developed, as a regular feature of their annual meetings, round table groups which provide opportunity for intensive discussion of rural social problems.

3. There has been a gradual increase in the number of papers on rural topics delivered at the National Conferences of Social Work, culminating in 1927 when one-fifth of the entire conference program was devoted to rural problems.

4. Since 1923 the American Country Life Association has sponsored a round table discussion on rural social work at the National Conference of Social Work, and has been instrumental in increasing the interest noted in the preceding paragraph.

5. Although we have made no attempt to measure it, there has been a noticeable and significant increase during this period in the number of articles on rural subjects appearing in the leading social work periodicals and journals.

PART II. PROBLEMS AND TRENDS

Prospects for the future, in so new a field as this, may best be discussed in terms of present trends and the problems which are discernable.

I. METHODOLOGY.

1. The present trend of opinion seems distinctly favorable to the development of a generalized type of social work adapted to the special needs of rural communities. The realization of this objective involves, however, the solution of several problems, the most important of which seems to be the following.

2. It has not yet been determined how broad a field of social technique can be successfully included in the equipment of a single worker. Various experiments in the combination of two or more programs under one county agent are now under way which should throw light on this problem during the next five years. More experimentation is needed.

3. In many states the development of rural social work is still largely under the auspices of an agency specializing in one phase of social work.

4. The training of social workers for the rural field is still given for the most part in schools whose traditions and environments are predominantly urban and specialized.

5. There is no widespread agreement as to the specific techniques which are needed to make indigenous rural social agencies adequately effective. There are two schools of opinion on this question,—the one favoring a substitution of a professionalized agency for the existing rural agencies, the other favoring supplementation of existing agencies by the professionalized agency.

6. There is no adequate basis for determining the extent to which the basic principles and procedures developed by urban social workers are applicable in rural situations.

II. ORGANIZATION AND ADMINISTRATION.

    1. The extension of the rural area occupied by professional social work may be expected to continue. The rate of expansion may, however, decrease.

        a. Less than half the rural area is at present occupied.

        b. The territory now occupied consists preponderantly of the larger and wealthier rural counties.

        c. The occupation of most of the remaining territory involves the solution of the problem of finding a practicable basis for organization in the smaller counties.

III. RESEARCH.

Among the problems in the field of rural social work which urgently need scientific study are the following:

    1. The economic, social, and personal bases of social maladjustment in rural communities. What are the causal factors in rural social madadjustment? How do they differ from those in urban social maladjustment? Are these causal factors increasing or decreasing in force? Is social maladjustment in rural communities likely to increase or decrease?

    2. The fitness of indigenous rural agencies for dealing with social maladjustment.

IV. TRAINING OF RURAL SOCIAL WORKERS.

    1. It seems probable that the next ten years will see more attention given to the training of social workers specifically for the rural field, although this trend might be affected by the outcome of such research as that suggested above.

    2. Particular attention will undoubtedly be given to the provision of practical rural experience in connection with the training of social workers for the rural field.

    3. There will probably be increasing provision of extension courses, institutes, and similar forms of training for social workers, public officials, and volunteer workers in rural communities.

    4. Perhaps the most important problems to be solved is the relation of state colleges of agriculture to the training of rural social workers. This problem is intimately connected with the possibility of combining social work with the farm and home demonstration services in smaller counties (referred to in Part II, Section II of this report) and

deserves very serious consideration. The demonstration workers are a better trained and better educated group, on the whole, than the rural social workers, and have more familiarity with rural life. At the same time there is some ground for doubting the permanent validity of the present program of demonstration work. In theory, at least, a combination of the two could be advantageous to both, and immensely so to the rural communities they serve.

V. DISCUSSION AND WRITING.

1. While the interest in rural social work manifested in state and national conferences of social work will undoubtedly continue to increase moderately, it would be unreasonable to expect any spectacular development along this line. The emphasis given to rural problems at the last National Conference of Social Work, in Des Moines, was a response to special circumstances and in no way indicative of what may be expected in the future.

   The present policy of the Committee on Rural Social Work is to stimulate the discussion of rural problems at state conferences through volunteer state agents who are appointed as members and state representatives of the Committee.

2. There is need for providing more opportunities for rural lay people to discuss the social problems about which they are concerned in the presence of experts who can make genuine contributions to the discussion. A hopeful trend in this connection is the apparently increasing interest among state conference and state-wide agency leaders in the organization of district or regional conferences in various parts of their respective states.

3. There ought to be considerably more discussion of social problems in the meetings, especially state and local meetings, of such organizations as the Grange, the Farm Bureau, Farm Women's Clubs, the cooperative associations, and at state Farm Weeks. Greater use should be made of expert social workers who can make genuine contributions to such discussions. In this field, too, there are encouraging signs, here and there, of an awakening interest in the treatment of social problems on the part of rural people and their organizations.

4. Perhaps the most important development that could take place in this area of our problem would be the development of an interest on the part of the rural press in the

scientific study and treatment of social maladjustment. That is not to say that the rural press is any less interested in the subject than the urban press. But we still hope for things in the rural press which we may have given up looking for in the urban press.

VI. SUMMARY OF MOST IMPORTANT PROBLEMS.

If we were asked to select from the preceding sections the four problems which seem most fundamentally important, we would select the following:

1. The determination of the bases of social maladjustment in rural communities.

2. The clarification of the future relationship between social work, on the one hand, and farm and home demonstration work on the other.

3. The development of a unified state wide approach to the development of rural social work in every state.

4. The development of an inquiring interest among rural editors in the study and treatment of social maladjustment.

CONCLUSION

We would like to say, in conclusion, that it must not be supposed because we social workers talk continually of social maladjustment, that we regard rural life as all maladjusted. On the contrary, it is because we perceive social and cultural values in rural life which we have all but given up hoping to restore to urban life, and because we fear that the same forces which have so nearly destroyed these values in urban life may destroy them also in rural life, that we are anxious to see these rural communities adequately equipped before the struggle becomes acute.

Leroy A. Ramsdell, *Chairman*

STATE REPRESENTATIVES

Grace Ashbaugh (N. E. Texas)
Jean Blanshard (Washington)
Abigail Brownell (Penn'a)
Anna M. Cameron (Nebraska)
Mame Camp (N. C.)
Grace Cary (Conn.)
Edward H. Cavin (Md.)
Louise Cottrell (Iowa)

Georgia Greenleaf (Mo.)
Charles F. Hall (Minn.)
Evadne Laptad (Kansas)
H. J. Mathews (Georgia)
Hannah Protzman (Ohio)
Mary Helen Smith (N. Y.)
A. H. Stoneman (Mich.)
J. H. Montgomery (Va.)

RURAL RECREATION AND SOCIAL LIFE*

GENERAL CONDITIONS

1. An important fact in this brief report is that almost everywhere within rural areas people have an unsatisfied desire for more play, recreation, and social life. This fact brings to the Committee the genuine thought of the rural folk to the forces of recreation. One of the most important discoveries of this generation is the value and importance of play in life. Do our rural people need release from monotony, tedious expressions of leisure time activity, and otherwise drab existences? Are they not being brought through play into creative freedom and a wider expansion of physical, mental, moral and social forces in life?

2. Another striking fact is the rapidly changing attitudes of rural folk toward play and recreation. The old attitude that play and recreation is wasted time or frivolous expenditure of energy or activity savoring of viciousness and sinfulness are fast disappearing. This is the most cheerful sign the committee can report. It is significant. It opens the way for us in the next decade to make advances in practical applications and programs to the limit of our ability.

3. The period has brought forth general agreement among rural sociologists that country recreation must be indigenous to country life and have a character of its own. If there be such a thing as "rural-mindedness" then it profoundly affects country recreation and every other detail of country life-social engineering, programs, activities, agencies and institutions involved in every type of social work in rural regions.

4. Plans for the organization of rural recreation have found little or no change from those methods given in the Report of the Committee on Recreation and Social Life of the American Country Life Association for the year 1920. The plans then enumerated were —a. Institutional plan; b, Inclusive recreation association or organization plan; c, Public-school direction plan; d, State and county cooperative plan; e, Community organization plan. (See the 1920 report for

*This report was drafted by Harold D. Meyer, University of North Carolina, Chairman.

78

explanations of these plans.) There are very definite trends to show tendencies drifting in favor of the fifth plan.

The problem of organization is still a big one. The county or political unit is giving way to community or neighborhood organization. The county does not adequately serve as a unit for the best development of play and recreation. These activities find no county bounds. They are limited only by community and neighborhool relationships. To express the plan and recreation movement as a part of the whole advancement of community life and to let it develop as community life advances seems to be the policy for the future.

5. Along with the problem of organization comes the problem of finance. As in the case of rural programs, hindrances have been found here. State support, county aid, philanthropical methods, institutional assistance and regional practices have all been tried—in some cases with success and in others with failure. There seems to exist a clear-cut tendency for the community or the neighborhood to assume its financial obligation and allow the many supplementary agencies and methods to aid. After all, the play movement or a wholesome recreation program can not be forced on people. It must come through realization of needs and values. Where these are realized, the financial problem is generally solved or made easier.

6. One of the most encouraging developments has been the attention given to the training of play and social leaders. Normal schools, agricultural colleges, universities and colleges, a few national agencies interested in play and recreation, and other independent, volunteer forces all include courses of study, conferences, instruction and training in play leadership. Emphasis has been given to the selection of volunteer leaders because much of the leadership for the small and scattered groups can be given by the volunteer.

7. Specific advances are most significant in the school. Consolidation of schools has helped most. The most hopeful agency solving the problem of rural recreation in America is the consolidated school. Play activities, playgrounds, equipment, athletic fields, auditoriums, play centers, festival programs, dramatics, music and most of the recreational forces have found their place in the consolidation movement. Certain legislative acts in regard to physical education in various states have brought about some activity.

8. Attention must be directed to the facilities making for easy contact with urban recreational practices and leisure-time pursuits. It would be difficult to estimate the advantages and disadvantages of these contacts. They are powerful in determining future ways of rural recreation. The psychology of the farmer and his family, the lack of country life, the sparsity of the country population, rural social in-

sulation, and so on, tend to call for other than urban methods. The Committee doubts that it is either possible or desirable bodily to transfer urban play methods to the open country.

9. The situation brought forth suggests the contributions made to rural recreation and social life through research institutes, graduate work in universities and colleges and investigations made by various agencies and foundations.

10. The large group of organizations, national, state, county and local interested in rural life and especially rural recreation and social life have contributed to advancement. The promotion of activities among rural boys and girls has been outstanding. The 4-H Clubs, Boy Scouts, Girl Scouts, Woodcraft League, Boy Rangers, Camp Fire Girls and a few others have added specific trends and values. At the present time emphasis is being given to adult activities. The parent-teacher movement, women's clubs, and many farm organizations are making rapid strides for promoting adult recreation and social life.

11. The last ten years has brought more and better literature on the subject. Led by the Playground and Recreation Association of America in its magazine *The Playground,* and developed by many other agencies, there is valuable information available for the better understanding of specific programs and the trends in rural recreation and social life. (The Committee or the Association office will furnish bibliographies or material on request.)

12. Many rural communities are in a stage between the pioneer days of individual sports and the days of community parties and socials of one kind and another. They will soon come into the time when definitely organized recreation programs will provide wholesome leisure-time activities.

Many rural regions are, however, still without evidences of awakening. Improvements and progress are not to be seen. In most every section of the country specific illustrations of this can be found.

The movement has been retarded in many places because of existing attitudes and difficulties prevalent throughout the history of the play movement. The attitudes and difficulties are disappearing and the new day with its scientific application, its enlarged program and its wider opportunity surely will find a way.

13. The rural church has shown little progress through the decade in meeting the recreation situation. In fact the United States over, the rural church is generally static, or on the decline. The hope seems to lie in consolidation and the Committee expresses the hope that the Church will soon catch the vision and bring to the rural community new forces of life.

SPECIFIC ILLUSTRATIONS.

1. *Home Play.*

a. Requests were sent to every agricultural extension division in the United States and to many national organizations interested in rural life. From the answers obtained only two states seem to be making a direct effort to bring the problem of home recreation for discussion among the rural people themselves. New York state holds leadership training schools for the construction of playground equipment and game leadership. West Virginia has listed in the community score card under "Home" a section pertaining to recreation in the home. They also have a discussion outline on home recreation which is used extensively by the farm women's clubs.

b. In the various publications a variety of activities are advocated in order to develop comradship between parents and children and for the enrichment of home life. Music is generally listed as the most important force to unify home life. Singing together leads the list. The radio and victrola however hold important places. Books and magazines are being read more. Story telling and dramatics are making slow but steady gains. The observance of home festivals has had a good influence. Hobbies of various kinds flourish in the homes where there is a spirit of comradship and they are usually found to have educational value. Bird study, raising pets, shop work, photography, museums and various handicrafts hold popular places.

c. Since relatively few of the rural people attend high school or college we must look to some of the newer movements in education to bring a fuller life to our rural homes. The plan that seems most adapted to rural community needs is the peoples' college plan, which has been patterned after the Danish folk schools. Here young people from eighteen to thirty may come together for a three-months period of study in a home atmosphere. Pocono Peoples College is probably the first of the American Peoples Colleges. It was established three years ago. At least three have been started and the movement promises to advance.

2. *Music.*

a. The vital use of music in the rural communities is a development still to be wished for rather than one that is already accomplished. However, there are many signs of encouragement. The radio and phonograph are being used in greater numbers every day and are exercising in the main a beneficial influence. So tawdry is poor music and so durable is good music that anyone who makes a practice of hearing music almost inevitably cultivates a taste for something which will stand the strain of continued use.

b.   When, however, we pass beyond the field of listening to music we are conscious of how much still remains to be done.   The singing in the country churches is still lamentably poor, and except in rather rare cases community singing at the usual social gathering scarcely exists.   Music in the rural schools has made a good start in many states, notably in Maine, Kansas, Iowa, and Wisconsin.   In these states careful procedures have been worked out.   With the aid of the phonograph, music can be taught effectively by even a teacher with little musical ability.   Publishers are becoming conscious of the possibilities of the rural schools and new books especially adapted to the needs of rural life are appearing.   The normal schools are improving the training of teachers who are to go out in the rural districts and this should mean the bettering of music teaching.   Some schools are putting in good equipment in phonographs and pianos and are definitely considering musical qualifications when engaging teachers.   In a few states some of the county supervisors are giving definite attention to music supervision.

c.   Up to the present very little has been done with instrumental work in the field of orchestra and bands for youths and adults in the country.   Living on isolated farmsteads is not conductive to the development of rural bands and orchestras.

d.   From the *Handbook of Rural Social Resources,* (University of Chicago Press) we find that "during the summer of 1924, the sum of $557,838 was paid by seven hundred 'fairs' for music programs.   The amount ranged from fifty dollars paid to a local band to $40,000 which was the cost to one fair association of engaging celebrated bands and noted singers and providing contests and prizes."   This handbook also tells of music contests that have proven stimulating to music appreciation.   In many states music festivals and state-wide contests are held.   Each year these events grow in interest and numbers.

e.   The educational work of the Victor Talking Machine Company is notable.   Other phonographic companies are doing work in this field.   They are also giving special attention to music in rural fields.

f.   The Eistedfod Movement in Southern California is an attempt to adopt a splendid Welsh institution to America.   The movement began in Ventura County through the community service organization in 1924 and consisted of a week of music, drama and art competition. Later the contests embraced all phases of music-elementary and high school groups, church choirs, community orchestras and so on.

g.   National Music Week has stimulated activity and interest. This week is sponsored by a large national committee on which rural interests are represented.   Through the cooperation of state and local groups the efforts of the committee are proving most successful.

h.   The universities and colleges of the country are doing a great deal to foster interest and programs.   This is especially true of the universities in the Middle West and the West.   Most of this work is promoted by extension divisions.   The University of Wisconsin radio program, the University of California concerts and lectures, the musical activities of the University of North Dakota, South Dakota, and Minnesota deserve mention.   The Playground and Recreation Association of America has published a number of bulletins and leaflets stimulating interest and giving aid in developing rural music activities.

3.   *Drama.*

a.   The significant activity in the field of drama has been the development of the folk drama.   Led by Fredrick H. Koch, director of the "Carolina Playmakers" and Alfred G. Arvold with the "University Players" in North Dakota the movement has spread to many universities and colleges.   A number of state dramatic associations have been established and are sponsoring contests and play producing activities.

b.   The Little Country Theatre idea is making headway and will continue its onward march for better play production, resources, costumes, plays, programs and suggestions for all types of entertainment in all types of places.   The attempt is to make the drama "not a luxury for the classes but an instrument for the enlightenment, self-expression and enjoyment of the masses."

c.   Work at Cornell University is outstanding.   In 1919, some European and American plays were given at the state fair in New York and the Little Country Theatre has become an important feature of the county fairs.   There were thirteen little country theatres at various fairs in 1920 and five more were added the next year and the movement is still growing.   The institution, like a number of educational institutions and extension divisions, is sponsoring contests for the best plays presented with the theme sympathetically portraying some phase of rural life.

d.   Many of the colleges of agriculture are sponsoring dramatic contests.   They are giving special attention to play festivals and pageantry.

e.   Religious drama has received great impetus through the development of assistants in denominations which sponsor activities of this kind.   The Federal Council of Churches of Christ in America has produced two volumes of religious drama and these are having wide usage.

4.   *Research.*

a.   H. L. Eels of Iowa State Teacher's College has made a study of what 1,300 college students and 168 high school students who came from the country do for recreation.

b.   Surveys have also been made by Warren H. Wilson, and by the Institute of Social and Religious Research, of the kind of recreation which rural young people prefer.   Surveys made of recreation and recreational facilities in Paulding and Gallia Counties, Ohio, brought out that there is a great lack of recreation among the rural people.

c.   Research might be undertaken under the Purnell Act to summarize the available data and material bearing on rural recreation. There is need for more research regarding the need for rural recreation and the extent to which it will bring about a greater contentment among rural people.

5.   *Organized Rural Activities.*

a.   Among the outstanding activities having recreational phases or values promoted by the 15 full-time and 3 part-time rural organization extension specialists were local leader training conferences; intertownship and county debates, which in some cases lead to state contests; monthly township or community meetings from which helpful material was furnished to enable local people to put on their own programs; rural orchestra contests; amateur dramatics; and country life conferences.

b.   The 4,500 county extension agents, supervisors and specialists assisted in promoting or conducting women's and boys' and girls' vacation camps, better educational exhibits, achievement days and special tours and events.   All of these have had done their major work during the past ten years.

c.   In planning recreation and in bringing out the advantages of any form of recreation, it is important that it be presented so as to appeal to people's desire for health, pleasure, comfort, commendation, gain, mental alertness and achievement.   These can all be provided for in planned fairs.

Fairs and exhibits furnish an important means for rural recreation which can be made of increased value to the people by providing for less commercial entertainment and more individual exhibits, contests, games, pageants, and plays in which a large number of people can participate.   There are more than 2,000 county fairs and more than 3,000 community fairs each year.   Exhibits are also put on at corn, apple, poultry and other shows.

d.   Two thousand, seven hundred and sixteen junior camps for boys and girls with an attendance of 211,025 members of the 4-H clubs, were conducted by county extension agents during 1926.   These are the principal vacation camps held for rural boys and girls, but similar encampments are conducted by the Y. M. C. A., the Y. W. C. A., the Boy Scouts and other organizations. In addition to the educational work taken up, these camps usually provide facilities for games, contests, swimming and athletic training. Such camps become one of the strong incentives for getting boys and girls to join the 4-H clubs. Some form of recreation is furnished at practically every meeting to more than 600,000 4-H club members under the direction of county extension agents and local leaders. County club rally days have been held in many counties.

e. There are about 117 county Y. M. C. A. secretaries who help to direct the recreational activities of rural boys. There are also about 40 rural Y. W. C. A. Secretaries who are recreation leaders for girls.

f. County vacation camps were held for farm women in 141 counties during 1926. These provide for a variety of recreation including the following: games, community singing, hikes, rest periods, homecraft training, music, demonstrations, folk dancing, swimming, tennis, ball games, boating, parades, home talent plays, pageants, debates and motion pictures. Many of the women who attended these camps have gone home with renewed energy and a new vision of their home responsibilities.

g. Rural pastor's and leader's training camps have been held. At least 2,000 pastors go to special summer schools yearly, and participate in recreation programs.

h. Achievement days have been held by hundreds of rural women's study groups for the purpose of bringing to the attention of the people of the county and community the achievements of the individuals, group or groups in the project work conducted in cooperation with the county home demonstration agents or home economics specialists. In Michigan, for example, 32 out of 39 counties carrying on home economics work on the local leader basis held such achievement days. Many original plays, poems, posters, and exhibits of finished articles, are prepared and presented on these occasions, affording the satisfaction of participation to many. Each township or community represented usually provides some program feature or number which takes about five minutes. An opportunity for exhibiting the best they have produced becomes one of the strongest incentives to produce quality products.

The Nebraska home demonstration leader reported that whereas the county-wide achievement days had an attendance ranging from 50 to 200 the first year, they had from 75 to 500 the second year.

6. *Special Tours and Festivals.*

a. Among the more important festivals conducted are the various apple and other fruit blossom festivals, sugar making, husking bees and

corn husking contests. A Kansas and a Missouri county have coop-
erated in conducting an apple blossom festival which has in three years
grown from a small tour and banquet to an enormous parade with two
miles of floats and decorated cars.

b. Hundreds of farm and home tours have been conducted by
the county extension agents in which a large number of rural people
participated.

c. A great many county and township picnics have been held at
which athletic, old fiddlers' and hog, chicken and husband calling contests have been conducted. A county-wide play day movement was
reported from Illinois for which play suggestions were developed for all
age groups. St. Louis County, Minnesota, held its third annual two
day recreational institute and gave training to one hundred and fifty
local leaders in recreational activities.

7. *Legislation.*

a. Pennsylvania is the first state in the nation to legislate for
county and township recreation and Chester County in that state was
the first county to take advantage of the legislation and provide
recreation on a county-wide basis under an officially appointed recreation board and a superintendent of recreation. The work is supported by county and township appropriations.

b. National, state and county park commissions have given impetus to wholesome recreation to rural as well as city folks. Such
conferences as The National Conference on Outdoor Recreation held
in Washington, District of Columbia, in 1925, and the Congressional
action in promoting parks in all sections of the United States have
found ready response and sympathetic interest.

While the Committee does not believe that wholesome play and
recreation is a panacea for all rural ills, it holds that there has been
a minimizing and a neglect of the values and functions of plays and
recreation. Sound in pedagogical principles, psychological procedure,
and sociological practice; carrying physical, mental, moral and social
values; possessing curative and preventive power, wholesome leisure-
time activities through organized play and recreation can add much to
the promotion of happiness and health for the rural folk in the days
ahead.

> Harold D. Meyer, *Chairman*
> A. G. Arvold
> Peter Dykema
> Betty Eckhardt
> Ralph A. Felton
> H. W. Gilbertson
> Alexander MacLaren

COMMUNICATION AND TRANSPORTATION*

The past decade has been one characterized by transition and experimentation in so far as communication and transportation in relation to rural life is concerned. Certain marked changes have influenced conditions a great deal but what those influences have been and what ultimate results they will bring about cannot be told to day. In the first place isolation, both physical and mental, is being eliminated, and the forces underlying communication and transportation are responsible for this fact. People dress alike all over the nation, and in fact, the civilized world. News that is of interest to New York City reaches the hills of West Virginia as quickly as New York gets it. Time and distance have almost been conquered by methods of communication and our transportation facilities are not far behind.

In the second place because of our conquests over distance the center of attraction in the rural areas is changing. In other words the community is replacing the neighborhood. If such terms are unsatisfactory, it may be said that the farm families desire better stores than can be found at the cross roads village so they can go to the small town. The automobile can travel ten miles as comfortably as a horse could travel three miles and so no time has been lost in searching for bette stores. The same is true of churches, schools, amusements, etc. The old centers have apparently lost their hold, and newer, bigger centers are taking their places. In many cases this is viewed with alarm, especially by those of the older generations who are still alive. They feel that the younger generations are of a roving nature and dissatisfied with conditions and this dissatisfaction is one of the causes of farm unrest and is chiefly responsible for many of the farm problems of today. Whether or not is has any direct bearing on our present day farm problems, the transition from the neighborhood to community is a direct result of our evolutionary methods in transportation and communication.

That the past decade has been one characterized by experimentation is certainly self evident when one glances over the list of new uses and methods employed in means of communication and transportation. The electrification of railways, introduction of truck and bus transportation, the commercial use of the radio, the commercial use of

*This report was drafted by T. A. Coleman, Purdue University, Chairman.

87

aviation, the new television idea applied to the telephone; all these and many more bring out emphatically the transitional condition of communication and transportation and under such conditions it is impossible to accurately assign causes and effects and just as futile to forecast. However, it is not impossible to point out danger spots and issue warnings and trust that these warning signs will be clear enough for those of the future to observe and heed. The report from hereon will confine itself to the special problems of communication and take them up separately.

Problems of Communication

The Telephone

According to the American Bell Telephone and Telegraph Company there are over three million rural telephones in the United States. The increase has been steady, the number of telephones having practically tripled in a period of twenty years. The census report shows almost 40% of all farms have telephones, there being less in the South than in the North. That the telephone renders a distinct service to rural life is shown by the functions it performs as enumerated by C. C. Taylor in his *Rural Sociology*, (Harper's). (1) Places the farmers in contact with each other in matters of business, protection, social organization, and visitation. (2) It places the farmer in touch with professional men of the city. (3) It places the farmer in touch with the market. (4) The rural telephone encourages cooperation.

The Radio

The radio, although a relatively new development, has had a tremendous growth in the last few years. The most recent survey of the United States Department of Agriculture shows that over one and a quarter million farm homes have radio sets, a gain of 126% over the number of sets estimated for July 1925. In as much as there is so much friction in regard to broadcasting, a great deal must be done before perfection is at all approached, but considerable has already been accomplished by the federal radio commission and the Department of Commerce.

Weather and market reports, music and other entertainment, world news, agricultural and other education, all are furnished to the farmer by the radio. Farm isolation is being relieved in many ways because of the radio and although the past has brought much, the future, in so far as the radio is concerned, holds in store even greater opportunities and pleasures for farm folks.

Books, Newspapers and Magazines

Books, newspapers and magazines have done much for the farm people in furnishing them with facts and keeping them in touch with the outside world. The free library has instituted the traveling section, which brings the book to the home. The country traveling library is reaching daily more and more homes and brings with it fiction and educational books. The libraries are growing and with the aid of the libraries and county agents farm people are reading more and more about the problems that so distinctly belong to the open country. Not only do they read of their own problems but through books the open country learns of the urban problems and the city learns of the rural problems and better understanding develops.

The newspapers carry the news, both local and national and in this way the farm people keep fully abreast of the times. Too few papers attempt to cater to the farm people, but are more apt to localize about the center of interest, notably the small town. Much can be done to increase the value of the rural newspapers but even so they are serving a useful purpose now.

Magazines, rural and urban, find their way to farm homes. A number of farm papers have a circulation of over one million copies. These papers devote themselves to rural problems and have the best authorities in the nation write for them. Other magazines, digests, reviews, those devoted to motherhood and the home, fiction, and many other subjects reach the farmstead as well as the city home. The United States Department of Agriculture as well as the state experiment stations send out millions of bulletins, circulars and articles for publication. With the passing of illiteracy has come an age of reading and with reading will come understanding.

Rural Free Delivery

The rural free delivery has continued to serve as it was intended. Mail comes to the farm home regularly each day. With the advent of the parcel post this type of mail also can reach the farm. The number of routes have grown until there are over 43,000. Over one million miles are covered by the carriers, almost 30,000,000 patrons served, while almost four billion pieces of mail were carried during 1920. The growth since then has been gradual and the service rendered enormous. An adjustment in routes is being made all the time in order to even better serve the farm families. Originally political influence caused some routes to be organized that were not capable of giving the best service. Gradually these have been and are being eliminated, and the keynote of the department is service.

Motion Pictures

The motion picture industry is playing an important part in rural communication. Contacts with the outside world are made here that could never be made without the aid of traveling. New lands are brought to the audience and all parts of the world are shown. Aside from this point of view the motion picture industry brings people together so that new contacts are made. Like books, magazines, newspapers and the radio it serves as a form of educational medium and Granges, Farm Bureaus, churches, schools, county agents and others make use of it for educational and recreational advancement.

The transition from neighborhood to community, mentioned in the beginning is leaving the village picture show, on the whole, a sorry institution. It cannot compete with theatres in larger centers, so shows old films and questionable ones, and has to, even if the manager were inclined to get better pictures. This recreational phase, not coming under the jurisdiction of this committee, is merely used here, to again illustrate, the inevitable change in rural life, the transition from a small to a larger center of interest.

Other Means of Communication

Nearly all the forms of transportation also become means of communication. The railways, the automobile, all of these things enable the farm people to come into closer contacts with each other and with the outside world. Education has done much to provide better facilities of understanding and the Extension Service of the Agricultural Colleges and Experiment Stations has brought millions of farm people in contact with each other and with the problems that involve farming. The Grange, the Farm Bureaus, the Farmers Union, all serve as a means of communication by bringing the farm people together to discuss problems or to enjoy some form of a recreational get-together.

Conclusions

No attempt has been made to cover all the details involved in the problems of communication and transportation. An effort has been made to give an idea of the development during the past decade and show the trend that most likely will be followed. Professor Hawthorne states that communication and transportation, as regards social progress, are equivalent to density of population. He further states that they mean the liberation from limitations of the locality or neighborhood. Unquestionably many of the advantages of the city are brought to the rural community and combined with the local advantages already present, make for ideal home surroundings. That progress has been made during the past ten years cannot be disputed. However, it is questionable whether the progress made was equal to the amount of potential progress available. Undoubtedly progress will be made during the next decade but with this progress will appear many undesirable features, unless they are hunted out and eliminated. Without some guidance, density of population, as brought to the rural community by communication and transportation, may carry with it the evils of the slums, rather than the benefits of the cultural centers.

On this account these new developments in communication and transportation must be carefully studied. Control must be exercised where control is needed. Trends must be anticipated and guided, rather than fought and forced into evils. And above all open mindedness must prevail, and the institution judged by the service rendered, not on a basis of prejudice and selfishness.

T. A. Coleman, *Chairman*
T. C. Horner
H. Keller
Guy Van Buskirk
George A. Von Tungeln

RURAL GOVERNMENT*

Rural government and rural organization have come in for serious consideration in a number of the programs of the American Country Life Association during the past ten years. The Committee on Rural Government has reported from time to time upon particular aspects of this large and increasingly important topic. A large measure of credit is due Dr. E. L. Branson of North Carolina for his efforts as Chairman.

Rural government in America is old in its establishment. It had its origin along with the early settlements before state and federal governments were existing. It is, therefore, closely entwined with the life of our people and has become intrenched with all the force of a nation's traditions. This furnishes evidence of why it is difficult to secure any change in organization even though the original function has disappeared or become devitalized.

The importance of this problem is graphically emphasized by the fact that nearly one-half of our population lives under the rural government and that the largest expenditure of money raised by taxation is found in the county government. In spite of these facts, the general public possesses less information and is less concerned about the rural government than any other unit. This is partially accounted for by the fact that so many of its functions seem far removed from the average citizen and his daily interests.

The Committee has devoted itself to urging certain fundamental needs. There is necessity for investigation in this field and study of the facts. Today the colleges and universities are giving little attention to the field. The situation calls for most serious consideration on the part of our educational leaders and authorities. In these days when rural interests are prominent our colleges ought to give greater emphasis to local government.

Again, the people living in rural areas seem indifferent to change. This is not surprising since they constitute our most conservative class. Their attitude is naturally quite in contrast with the attitude of their brother the city dweller who lives in an atmosphere of change.

Even a cursory knowledge of the field of rural government gives abundant evidence of the difficulties of remedying the evils. It is

*This report was drafted by E. H. Ryder, Michigan State College, Chairman.

apparent that present governmental areas are artificial and not coincident with any natural functional expression. For instance we insist on the township as a unit in the administration of justice in spite of the fact that the problems which a justice of the peace must handle have entirely changed. Furthermore, we find large numbers of people governmentally segregated when they possess no interest in common. It is obvious that the situation demands an adjustment whereby people will be grouped according to some real interest. The committee has brought before the Association information bearing upon this problem showing how many of our states are really seeking new lines of demarcation into natural functioning areas.

These needs receive recognition in recent laws in Wisconsin, Michigan and North Carolina. These states are pioneering, and are pointing the way to some modifications of the local rural organization for the purpose of greater efficiency in local rural functions, as well as to render more service through existing organizations.

If any judgment is to be voiced at this time, it is that the merits of the subject have scarcely been recognized in the past ten years of the Association programs, and it is to be hoped that in the years to come time may be found for more emphasis upon this great topic together with its companion subject of the obligations of citizenship by the residents of our land.

E. H. Ryder, *Chairman*
Benjamin Shambaugh
Griff Johnson
E. C. Branson
W. L. Bailey
Miss Elliott

TAX LEGISLATION*

By Charles L. Stewart,

University of Illinois

Chief, Department of Agricultural Economics, University of Illinois

We are apparently standing in the early dawn of the morning after so far as important reforms in our Federal taxation is concerned. Whatever legacies of a good or bad type which the decade begun by our entrance into the World War left us, the one to which I refer seems to be so definitely good that it must prove to be a thorn in the side of the pessimists. I am now about to quote. In the years immediately preceding the World War more than 90 percent of Federal tax receipts "came from indirect taxes, customs duties, and taxes on articles of domestic consumption, largely tobacco products and alcoholic beverages. Now, although receipts from customs and from miscellaneous internal revenue are larger than in pre-war days, these sources are of minor importance compared with the income taxes paid by individuals and by corporations. Indirect taxes, the burden of which is distributed rather generally among the consuming public, have been largely replaced by taxes on the income of individuals, graduated according to the sizes of the income, and by taxes on the income of business."

This quotation from the 1926 report of the Secretary of the Treasury refers to a change in Federal taxation the full meaning of which has not yet come home to many. The fact is that there has been both an evolution and a revolution in our Federal taxing system. The evolution has been away from dependence on the tariff and the revolution has been toward dependence on income taxes. The evolution has been progressing throughout several periods of our history. The revolution came suddenly and recently.

Consider first the evolution as a result of which the tariff has been largely displaced as a source of Federal revenue. Consider the contrast between the first four years of the American tariff, 1791-1794, and the last four years. During the recent quadrennium the tariff produced 130 times as much money for the treasury as during the first four years. At the same time, however, compared with other sources of Federal revenue the tariff is only one-seventh as important as during that earlier period. In other words, the tariff produced but

*From Address at Eleventh National Country Life Conference.

a little more than four million dollars a year 135 years ago, but is now producing over 600 million dollars a year. Nevertheless, during the earlier period 95 percent of all the Federal revenues were derived from the tariff, whereas in the last few years less than 15 percent has been so derived.

During the last 75 years the percentage of total receipts of the Federal treasury represented by tariff revenues declined 80 points, or more than one percentage point a year. At this rate the tariff would disappear altogether as a source of treasury revenues by 1940.

It is possible to state the extent of change of dependence upon the tariff in even more emphatic language. In 1791 the proportion of total ordinary receipts supplied by the tariff was nearly 100 percent, or to be exact, 99.6 percent. In 1919 the proportion was 3.9 percent. This is a change almost without parallel in the case of any other source of Federal funds. Had the amount of revenue receipts from the tariff continued to decline in the nine years after 1919 as in the nine years before, the tariff produced for the present year would be, not 600 million dollars, but less than 50 million dollars. If the proportion which tariff revenues were of all Federal receipts had declined after 1919 as during the nine years preceding, the tariff would have disappeared as a revenue producer in 1920.

All of this is said in full recognition of the fact that our 600 million dollar tariff of the last two years is twice as productive as the tariff was during the years immediately preceding our entry into the World War. Nevertheless, a tariff producing between one-half and two-thirds of a billion yearly is producing only about one dollar in seven drawn into the United States Treasury.

The virtual elimination of the tariff as a dominating factor in Federal revenues has had three important stages. The first one extended through the first half of our constitutional history, that is, to the time of the Civil War. During this stage the tariff was producing over 80 percent of the Federal revenues practically every year.

During the period between the Civil War and the World War the tariff was rather regularly the source of half of the Federal receipts. Miscellaneous internal revenues, largely levied on alcoholic beverages, tobacco, playing cards, etc., were the almost exclusive dependence for the other half of Federal revenues during this period.

Now we are in the third phase, tariff receipts constituting by no means a negligible, but by all odds a relatively small proportion of the total revenues.

The recent subsidence of the tariff to its lowly position as a revenue producer was made possible by the change by which income and business taxes were suddenly thrust into larger importance in our Federal system. Whether we shall continue to have over 50 percent of our Federal revenues derived by taxation of income or whether there may be an expansion of tariff revenues and miscellaneous internal taxes to such an extent as to decrease the relative importance of income taxes seems to be a matter requiring not much debate. A tendency to make the tariff more effective with regard to our imports, quite apart from any export policies that may be adopted, may prevent the tariff from yielding more at present. On the other hand, the tendency away from excise taxes seems to persist from one revenue act to the next and may continue to reduce the proportion of Federal revenues from these sources.

The possibility that income taxes will yield from two-thirds to three-fourths of the Federal revenue seems rather strong during the decade immediately before us.

Such trends in Federal taxation may be said in general to be highly desirable from the standpoint not only of agriculture but of our general economic life. By this I do not mean to infer that tariff duties so high as to be prohibitive and therefore productive of no income are preferable to duties less prohibitive. Nor is it to be inferred that some taxes on sales of commodities and some taxes on luxurious amusements may not have a legitimate place in Federal taxing of a more helpful sort. On the whole, however, the support of the activities of the Federal government seems destined to rest upon incomes of persons and of business on a basis of graduation and exemption that makes that load relatively light so far as persons of small income are concerned.

The shift which has been described has brought a conflict between the traditional and the revised ideas as to what Federal subsidy signifies. The traditional idea of subsidy as it came to us from England and as it persisted pretty much unchallenged until the World War is that of a combination of treasury appropriations, on the one hand, and special taxes, on the other. An example holding true to the old English traditions was afforded by Sir John Russell when, addressing our College of Agriculture recently, he pointed out that agriculture research and extension is supported in England by a tax on whiskey levied especially for that purpose. This exemplifies subsidy, for it is a combination of special taxes with treasury appropriations of the proceeds of such taxes. It involves a special burden imposed, on the one hand, in order to confer a special benefit, on the other.

The traditional or old English idea of subsidy was modified so far as our Federal system is concerned so as to omit the requirement that special taxes be levied. Any beneficiary of Federal appropriations was subsidized even though the appropriations were made, as they always must be under our Federal system, from the *general* rather than *special* funds. So long, therefore, as Federal funds were mainly derived by taxes on imports, on the one hand, and on the other hand, taxes on beverages, playing cards, tobacco and certain other items largely associated with the indulgences or relaxations of the people, it is little wonder that subsidy came to be associated with popular distaste. To appropriate Federal money even for plausible purposes seemed to involve, in the days preceding the World War, the introduction if not of new taxes certainly of more burdensome tax rates.

It can hardly be expected that popular distaste must continue to be associated with Federal appropriations as during the years preceding the World War. The fact that subsidy is not what it used to be places upon our people an obligation to be discriminating in their judgments as to what are desirable benefits and what are tolerable burdens. The fact that these burdens fall primarily upon persons of large income, whereas the benefits are distributed largely upon persons below the exemption limits indicates something of the scope of the temptations toward exploitation of the few at the hands of the many which is a possibility now found in our Federal system practically for the first time.

Will succeeding revenue acts continue to raise exemptions in a manner corresponding to that which was done in the revenue act of 1926? In that case, according to the report of the Secretary of the Treasury, personal exemptions were increased so as to free from tax about 3,400,000 taxpayers in the lower income brackets. In addition the credit for earned incomes was increased. In this particular case, to be sure, reductions were made in the rates of surtax on incomes in the higher brackets. The fact that experience seems to show that such surtax rates tend to fail of revenue production when approaching too close to the half-way point are too far beyond it, will doubtless continue to hold in bounds any tendency to throw the entire burden of Federal taxation upon persons of the very largest incomes. Nevertheless, in the support of our national government we are experimenting with the exemption of the masses to an extent without parallel in the history of countries supporting their national measures by income taxes.

Exemptions from taxes, remissions of taxes and credits for taxes are features which must be reappraised in the light of the new complexion of Federal taxation. Striking examples are afforded by securities issued by municipalities to raise funds for community improvements, as well as by other issues of tax-exempt securities, whether exempted as to principal or income and whether exempted as to Federal, state or local taxes. The exemption privilege is sold and made transferable in such securities. The first buyer pays for the privilege of exemption and the community obtains more funds on a bond on which it pays a given rate, or obtains a par amount of funds on a bond on which it pays a sub-

standard rate.   Future buyers of the same security may pay more or less
that the first buyer, depending on conditions.   If the tax rates decline,
the exemption is worth less; if they advance the exemption is worth
more.   Obviously the purchaser of tax exemption stands to gain if tax
rates are not reduced, and to lose if they are.   Holders of tax-exempt
securities seldom receive all of their income from such securities and
are as much concerned to have lower rates on their non-exempt income
as to have rates continue high on their exempt incomes.   In fact, it
appears that persons of the largest incomes have placed a smaller proportion of their income on an exemption basis than persons of medium
large incomes.   In any case, exemptions of a transferable kind are a
part of our Federal income-tax system and may be expected to continue.

Constitutional amendments proposed to abolish such exemptions
seems to be doomed to failure.   The basic reason for such a view is
that the Federal government cannot be given the right to tax income on
state securities without granting state governments the right to tax
incomes on Federal securities.   If states, however, are given the right to
tax Federal securities, any state desiring to obstruct the prosecution of
a war or other Federal enterprise could do so by making the tax position
of Federal securities unfavorable in that state.   Secession from the
financial prosecution of a Federal enterprise cannot be tolerated as a
legal right of any state or group of states.

Transferable tax exemption, therefore, seems to be a fixture rooted
in our system of political jurisprudence.   Its goodness or badness as a
fundamental practice is not to be brought into argument.   Here is one
case in which constitutionality cannot be waived.   The tax is the only
thing that can be waived.   Our concern must be to examine the exemptions to see whether in the case of each proposal, the exemptions increase burdens in the wrong quarters and increase benefits in the right
quarters.

The right to tax, we often say, is the right to destroy.   The power
to tax, as conferred by constitutions, carries the implicit power to
exempt from taxation, to waive taxes, to give credits for peculiar features surrounding the tax.

Tax-exempt farm loan bonds are apparently rationally adjusted to
public needs.   Credits for earned incomes so as to lighten the burden
on a given amount of income resulting from personal exertion as compared with income from property, are apparently taking a place also
as a feature of rational adjustment.   Other credits, exemptions and
waivers are being proposed and tried.   The problem is to keep the movement proceeding rationally.

A rational approach to the problem of exemptions requires a distinction between exemptions made under a system of taxation in which

income taxes have a large place and those made under systems in which the main dependence is on general property taxes. This brings us to the situation in most of our states. Exemptions in non-income-taxing states have a somewhat different relation to public welfare from exemptions in income-taxing states.

Consider, for example, the exemption from taxation of publicly owned public utilities. Exemptions from state business taxes in the case of publicly owned gas and electric utilities and public owned railroads in California were recently estimated to have reduced the receipts of the state treasury about one and one-half million dollars. The exemption of these same enterprises and their securities from Federal taxation amounts to about half as much. In this one state apparently the business tax produces less than 96 percent of its full capacity by virtue of the exemption of publicly owned public utilities. Obviously here is a problem in rural-urban relations inasmuch as this form of tax exemption, through public ownership, exists almost entirely within cities. Persons living in urban districts are thus enabled to receive benefits in the form of low-cost utility service, while the non-exempt real estate, much of it agriculture, has to carry a larger proportion of the state tax burden. Owners of farm property in such circumstances are likely to be found among those who may be lacking in enthusiasm for public ownership of public utilities in which they and their property can be credited with receiving only indirect benefits, if any at all, in offset to the increased relative burden upon their realty.

A similar example of the encroachment of public property upon the tax base is afforded in rural New York. Land acquired by the state for purposes of afforestation has been withdrawn from the tax lists of the respective townships and counties, tending to increase the burden upon other land, thereby increasing the tendency for the other land to escheat to the county or state, and in turn be added to the public area. Thus the process of public purchase of real estate tends to tilt the plane so as to cause still other real estate to slide out of the hands of private owners. As Professor G. F. Warren puts it:

"Any sound taxation policy must consider the other land as well as the forest land.

"Whatever agency takes over such land, provision must be made for the maintenance of such local institutions are are still required. Some roads may be closed. In many cases an entire school district may be completely depopulated. In come cases, townships should be combined. But many of the roads would still be needed, and local government and education must continue. If the poorest land is freed from taxation, and the entire burden thrown on the next poorest land, it amounts to confiscation of the remaining land that might be used for farming.

"If a portion of the land is removed from taxation and a corresponding reduction cannot be made in services, provision must be made to maintain the necessary local services."

This we may regard as the first feature in a rational use of the exemption principal in local areas or in states where exemption relieves a portion of the tax base only to burden more severely the portion that is left.

A second point in rationalizing our use of the exemption principal is to apply it so as to conserve natural resources. This has both a Federal and a state application. Consider first the effect of the conservation principal in respect to Federal import duties. Import duties levied so as to elevate the domestic price of minerals of which the supply is limited in the United States stand in a different position from import duties administered so as to raise the price of farm products. Reproducible products of growth must be given a separate consideration from exhaustible products of mines and forests. Policies tending to shut off importation of exhaustibles or to stimulate their exportation may easily prove to be shortsighted. The reason is that reduced imports of such products now or stimulated exports now merely pave the way for increased imports in the next few decades. If any export policy were to be needed in the case of exhaustibles it would be one of taxation of exports rather than stimulation. Certainly, it would be of doubtful wisdom for our exports of petroleum, for example, to be permitted for any considerable period to exceed our imports of that product.

Quite the reverse may hold in the case of products of short-cycle growth, such as farm products. To tax the exportation of such products is not desirable in the public interest. Formal taxation of exports of any kind is prohibited by the constitution. The recent reduction in the power which our agricultural exports have to command imports in exchange, however it may be likened to that which might have resulted from a formal export tax could not be the result of such a policy in this country. Whatever method may be employed for increasing the power of exports to command imports in exchange, and several have been suggested, such as adjustment favorable to agricultural exports need not conflict with the principle of conservation of our natural resources. A revival of the export branches of American agriculture would not be likely to result in soil exhaustion. In fact, it appears that soil has suffered more depletion during depression that a return of prosperity to its holders could be expected to restore in several years.

The conservation principle does not need to be brought into the taxation field by any forcible means. The fact is that it is essential to logical tax policy. A tax which tends to destroy its own base is objectionable on grounds of sound taxation as well as on social grounds. Such a tax, in the words of Adam Smith, "While it obligates the people to pay may thus diminish or perhaps destroy some of the funds which might enable them more easily to do so." Or, to use the words of a recent Under-Secretary of the Treasury, "the most important principle of taxation is, then, a tax system that will preserve and not destroy the sources upon which it feeds."

The conservation of natural resources, however, requires marked adjustments in our state and local methods of taxing and exempting from taxes. Our tendency to base assessments upon selling valuations rather than upon annual values, as expressed in rent, net returns, or some other such criterion, is here brought into question.

Some have gone so far as to urge that assessments no longer be made on estimated selling price, but that the income method be grafted into the property tax system, at least so far as productive property is concerned. Taxing real estate, for example, on its rent rather than on its selling price is an application of the conservation principle that readily suggests itself. The burden upon mining property, timber land and farm land would seem to be thus rendered more subject to fluctuation in accordance with changes in the gross or net amount of value produced from such property. Thus the pressure to keep production from mines, forests or fields running high would be tempered. The relaxing user or the holder who might wish to postpone the development of his mining property, his timber land or his farm would suffer less for his slower pace.

The principle of conservation of natural resources cannot be permitted, however, to result in the encouragement of human idleness or easygoing speculation in property ownership. Speculation that is rather disciplinary in effect may always be needed, but that which is gone into and out of on too easy terms is not for the public to encourage. Wherever the attempt to graft the net income idea into real estate assessment is likely to encourage speculation in farm land a basis for objection arises. A study of information collected in 1920 indicated that farm land was being held for rents as low as two percent of the selling valuation in some parts of the country and for rents as high as eight or ten percent of the selling valuation in other parts. Even within the same state rents which might seem to justify a valuation of a hundred dollars an acre in some sections would presumably have justified acre valuations of two hundred dollars or more in others. Where land held high in valuation in spite of low annual returns is required to join with land of higher annual returns but no higher selling valuation in the support of state or county expenditures, resort to the land-income basis of assessing the real estate would penalize the less speculative holders and favor the more speculative holders. Wherever a large proportion of our real estate is held speculatively or semi-speculatively, it appears that the European methods of taxing on annual values may be of doubtful applicability.

Nevertheless, selling valuation cannot be followed in the case of lands bearing exhaustibles, such as oil and minerals, or semi-exhaustibles, such as trees, without some mitigation. In the case of such properties the speculator who refuses to throw upon the market the largest amount of product possible in any short period may be serving the public good. His foresight may tend to reduce current wastefulness and prolong domestic supply. How much to mitigate the tax burden on such properties in the interest of a slower schedule of exploitation is not an easy problem. Where tax relief on one class of property must necessarily increase the burden on another class of property, it is a matter of great difficulty to apply the principle of conservation.

Without recourse to income taxes to take up the slack resulting from such tax relief the problem is practically hopeless in most states. With a broad basis of income taxation, however, taxes adjusted to the relief of specific classes of property can be practical.

In the case of local rates in England assessment of real estate is one-fourth as high for a given annual valuation of agricultural property as for the same annual valuation of urban property. Even with a lofty appreciation of the place of agriculture in national, state and local economy, however, there are few parts of the United States in which such discrimination would be regarded as tolerable by owners of urban property. "Uniformity" clauses are in our constitutions and have great tenacity. So great a degree of tax relief for agricultural property in our states is utterly impossible except as state taxes on personal and business incomes may give it possibility by avoiding what would otherwise be the necessity of throwing a corresponding increase in the tax burden on urban real estate and other property.

The transformation in Federal taxation which marked the past decade or more has opened up new grounds on which to judge the propriety or impropriety of Federal taxes, Federal tax credits, exemptions and waivers. Any such corresponding change in state taxation can hardly come with such swiftness and must certainly lack uniformity from one state to another. One can at least inquire whether the next few decades will find systems of taxing personal and business incomes in our states opening up new grounds on which to judge the propriety or impropriety of state and local general property taxes such as have come down from the nineteenth century and before.

It is difficult to apply a principle of conservation of the natural resources of the nation by irregular action on the part of 48 taxing states.   The fact that the principle is not yet well applied in the case of Federal tax policies does not add to the comfort of the situation. Nevertheless, our people are thinking about the use of taxing and tax waiving in more fundamental terms than in previous generations. For a democracy such as ours to think is a guarantee that gains already made will not be easily surrendered and other gains will be earnestly pursued.

In any event, it is not rational for state tax policy to over burden lands bearing exhaustible natural resources.   The same lack of rationality attaches to any taxing policy, state or Federal, which unduly stimulates the exhaustion of resources the practical end of which will mean premature dependence on supplies conserved in other countries.

BENEFITS FROM TAXATION*

M. H. HUNTER,

Department of Economics, University of Illinois

I have been to two places where there was no sign of merriment to counteract the general gloom which prevailed. One place was a funeral and the other was at the tax-gatherer's window. So general was the depression of spirits that even the undertaker and the tax-gatherer seemed to have acquired a sympathetic attitude. Many of you have attended funerals and have paid taxes, and I wonder if you have not felt about the same in both cases. In one case you are departing from a friend forever, and in the other it is departing forever from some good, hard-earned cash.

I have paid taxes for several years, but two years ago I was so annoyed by them that the culmination was a rather interesting experience that I want to relate to you. The day had been a trying one. I had paid the taxes on my house and lot and on my small amount of personal property that I could not hide from the assessor. My lawyer had informed me that he had succeeded in adjusting the small estate that my uncle had left me, but that one-third of it would be absorbed in taxes to the federal and state governments. I took my wife to the matinee and had to pay a tax on the tickets. The new car which I had ordered was delivered in the evening, and the dealer told me that more than $100 of the cost was a tax. I took my family for a ride, and had to pay two cents a gallon tax on the gas I bought. After dinner I went to the club to find a tax of ten percent added to my dues and a letter from the internal revenue collector informing me that my income tax return was past due and that a penalty would be added.

Is it any wonder that I went home early, and that I thought "taxes"? I retired but could not sleep, so turned on the light to read my favorite magazine until my nerves regained some semblance of equilibrium. As I glanced through it, is it any wonder that an article entitled "A Land Without Taxes" arrested my attention? As I read I discovered that the island of Trinigonia, one of the Philihama group, was a land without taxes. Here the inhabitants live, and move, and have their being, yet are never disturbed by the tax-gatherer. No

*From Address at Eleventh National Country Life Conference.

104

assessor makes an annual visit to question concerning one-s property, and no income tax returns are ever made. No tax is unintentionally paid in purchasing a cigar or openly paid with club dues or in purchasing a theatre ticket.

Here was the possibility of escape from the distasteful task of paying taxes, and since we had been planning a year abroad, it did not take me long to make up my mind that it would be spent in Trinigonia. I was even joyous when I announced to my family that we were going to spend the year in a land without taxes. Business matters were adjusted as quickly as possible and we were off on our new venture. And when the next full moon took her place in the eastern horizon we were comfortably located in one of the cities of the new land. The voyage had been one of peace and calm, but the calm was such as comes before a storm.

We had been there but a few days when I picked up the morning paper and was startled by an article on the front page. It indicated that tribute was about to be exacted by one of the neighboring countries. My pulse quickened and my blood warmed as I thought, "Millions for defense, but not a cent for tribute"—an expression I had heard my grandfather use years before. I rushed to the street to find if someone could explain the situation to me.

An old citizen, to whom I expostulated in no uncertain terms, appeared the very quintessence of calmness as he explained that such things had happened, and might be expected to happen again.

"But why do you permit it? Why don't you protect yourselves with your army and navy? It is preposterous! A disgrace!" I exclaimed, becoming still more excited.

"Stranger, calm yourself, and I will explain," he interrupted. "The army and navy? Such institutions are unknown in Trinigonia. To have such would necessitate a tremendous burden upon our people. In a country called the United States of America, they tell me, there has never been a year in which the federal government has not spent more for the army and navy than for any other item.

"Besides," he continued, "the maintenance of armies and navies may lead to war and wars in these days are expensive pastimes. Not only is their cost in lives and materials almost incomprehensible while they are in progress, but they place burdens upon future generations which can scarcely be removed. Let me show you what the World War did.

"The World War," he continued, "placed a per capita burden of indebtedness of about $225 upon the citizens of the United States. This means that in order to meet the interest charge and the payment of the debt by the plan they have adopted, it will require that about two percent of the entire annual income annually be collected in taxes. Yet I have no doubt that there is much agitation for lower taxes. In other countries the burden is still greater. In Great Britain the annual charge upon the social income is ten percent, while in France, Germany, and Italy it is much greater."

He dismissed the subject by saying that he believed there were advantages in the policy they pursued. I returned, somewhat ill at ease for the safety of the country, pondering the information I had received.

As I entered the door my wife excitedly informed me that her fur coat and hand bag had been stolen. I rushed out to notify the police. Imagine my surprise when, less than four blocks away, I met a man walking leisurely along with the coat over his arm. I stopped him, demanded the coat, and threatened to call the police.

"Call the police?" he replied with a sneer, "G'wan and call 'em. There ain't none here. That's the reason I'm here. Police made it too hot for me in New York, so I came here where there ain't no money to pay police. This fur coat is yours if you are man enough to take it."

With a sneer, he was on his way and I did not molest him. I started back but noticed fire breaking out on a nearby roof. I rushed to the corner to turn in an alarm and could find no box. I next rushed to a telephone and asked the operator to connect me with the fire company, only to be curty informed that there was no such subscriber.

The situation was forced upon me. Protection to person and property must here be provided by the individual. A reliable pistol would soon be cherished among my cherished possessions, and that evening I looked through magazines for advertisements of firearms. An article entitled "The Harshness of Governments" caught my eye. A part of it was instructive:

"In some countries," is stated, "the government has so little regard for its citizens that it taxes them in order to furnish protection, which in our country each citizen provides for himself. In the United States of America large sums are exacted for this purpose. The cities maintain a police force at great cost, and purchase expensive apparatus to fight fire. The cities alone annually spend nearly five dollars per capita for protection. When the amounts spent by the federal and state governments are added to this, the resulting tax burden is appalling."

I retired, pondering the relative effectiveness of protection in Trinigonia and the United States.

On my way to the park the next morning I stopped at the post office to get a card. The clerk charged five cents, against which price

I complained. He replied that they were in business for profit, and since they were a monopoly the price would be placed where the profit would be the greatest. Occasionally, he pointed out, as in the United States, the postal system is conducted at a loss, so that the rates may be low, but that such a plan would be impossible here.

At last I reached the park. It was privately owned and managed. I paid twenty-five cents for admission, ten cents to sit on a bench, and one dollar for a bathing suit and admission to the pool. Everything was so unsatisfactory that I soon left, still more enlightened as to conditions in a land without taxes.

New experiences came thick and fast, I soon encountered a man such as I had never seen before. His large physique, scraggy beard, long hair, and piercing eyes made a spectacle not soon to be forgotten. For ten minutes he compelled me to listen to his harangue about the wonderful civilization on the moon. I made my escape to assist a little girl who had fallen in an epileptic spasm. And just as I turned to go a ragged cripple begged for money.

"Why aren't these individuals where they should me?" I said to myself. Just then a minister with whom I had become acquainted came along, and I complained to him about the crime of allowing such defectives and paupers to intermingle with society. He wished it might be different, then proceeded to tell me of the cost of such institutions in the United States.

To my surprise I learned that the federal government ordinarily spends more than half as much in caring for the defectives, delinquents, and dependents as it does for protection to person and property. In the states, only one item, education, receives a greater expenditure, while in nearly one-fifth of the states the cost of public institutions ranks first. When the expenditures of cities and counties are added, the total cost of caring for these classes of human culls is really appalling, placing an annual burden upon the tax payers of about $400,000,000.

The issue was closed. I walked on with spirits somewhat depressed. And in such a frame of mind it is little wonder I hastily accepted the invitation of a neighbor to join him on a motor trip. I remembered the exhilaration I had experienced from speeding over the concrete roads of Illinois at forty miles an hour.

We were in his Duplex roadster. But the trip was a disappointment from beginning to end. There was no concrete nor asphalt. Toll gates and toll bridges were frequent, and more than once we had to be pulled from mud holes. I complained about the deplorable conditions and in contrast pictured the highways of the United States.

"You have forgotten," said my friend with an approach at a smile, "that you came from a country where the government performs functions, among which is the building and maintenance of highways. In Trinigonia, however, they must be provided by individuals. The receipts from tolls constitute their earnings, and it is not profitable to build expensive roads and to keep them in good condition."

I needed no further evidence why Trinigonia was a land without taxes. That night, after the children had retired, I told my wife that my curiosity was satisfied, and that I was ready to leave. Personally, her feelings were the same as my own, but she raised the question of the children's education. It was nearly time for school to open. John was to be a junior in college, Bob a sophomore in high school, and little Mary was eagerly looking forward to her first day in school.

My wife was right. The education of the children should not be disturbed. My mind had been so occupied that I had not been concerned about educational facilities. On the morrow I decided to investigate them.

The results were far from satisfactory. Primary education was given in private schools where the teachers were made to meet no particular requirements. High school subjects were taught, either by a private tutor or by several individuals combining to hire an instructor. The cost of enrollment in the primary school was $350.00 a year, while a tutor would cost about $500.00.

I remarked at dinner, after we had discussed what I had discovered, that I wished I knew something of the colleges.

"Well, dad," said John, "I fear it will be an expensive proposition. There seem to be only two institutions that can really be called colleges. Their annual tuition is about $1,000. Again I pay for room and board my year will cost between $2,000 and $2,500.

"Well, doesn't that beat you!" I exclaimed. "Some difference between your last year's tuition of $50, and $1,000. How do you account for it, anyhow?"

"Well," said John, "the situation set me to thinking, and when I found this book on educational costs in Johnson's library, I decided to bring it home. The charge for the book is twenty-five cents a day— think of it—when at home I could get all the books I wanted for the asking."

I took the book, glanced through it, and read the following passages:

"All countries do not look upon education in the same light. In some the benefit is considered as accruing entirely to the recipient, and the entire cost is borne by him. This idea is followed in Trinigonia.

"Some countries assume the attitude that education so increases the efficiency of its citizens that it is a great public good. The particular benefit to the individual is often not considered, for the rich bachelor may be taxed more heavily to maintain educational facilities than the poor man with several children in school.

"In the United States the public expenditure for education is tremendous. Primary education is not only gratuitously provided but its acceptance is made compulsory. Normal schools are provided to train teachers, secondary education is made attractive and inviting at no cost, while a large number of universities have been established where only a small fee is charged the student.

"The large expenditure for education is not confined to any political unit. The federal government gave vast tracts of public lands to foster its development, and continues to spend no inconsiderable sum. In the states no other item is emphasized to such an extent, while in the cities more than one-fifth of the total expenditure is for education."

"Well," I said, as I returned the book, "I see another reason why this is a land without taxes."

Mary went to the Smith school for beginners, and a private tutor was secured for Bob. I decided to go to Collegeville, about a hundred miles distant, to help John get comfortably located.

"Two to Collegeville," I said as I stepped to the ticket window.

"Fourteen twenty," said the agent as he stamped the tickets.

"I want only one-way tickets," I said.

"That is what I am giving you. A single fare is $7.10; two make it $14.20."

"Seven-ten," I said as I pulled out another billI. "I never heard of such fares; why, its more than seven cents a mile."

We boarded the train. The coach was dirty and poorly ventilated. An intoxicated man was making himself generally obnoxious. I noted the absence of any safety appliances and spoke to John of the contrast between this railroad and its equipment and the ones at home.

John exclaimed that in the United States transportation is closely regulated by government commissions. These not only fix the rates, but require many safety appliances and certain standards of service. And immediately I saw that taxes had been responsible for a part of the railroad service to which I had been accustomed. The size of the monthly telephone, light, and gas bills which I found in the mail when I reached home were still other evidences of the absence of regulation.

A few evenings later Mary came home sick, with the information that many of her schoolmates were home because of sickness. A physician was called and diagnosed the case as one of typhoid. The epidemic, he explained, came from polluted water, and it was somewhat regular in its recurrence. He was sorry that no preventive measures could be undertaken, but there was no one to do it.

Then it forcefully struck me that we were not paying taxes to secure health and sanitation. Typhoid might be followed by small pox or yellow fever. The risk was too great. As soon as Mary was well enough, we would embark for the United States.

The day before our departure I went to the bank to close my account. Here I was to have the last reminder that I had been sojourning in a land without taxes. The bank had failed because there had been no government regulation. I received but forty cents on the dollar. I purchased tickets in haste, and the happiest moment of my stay in Trinigonia was when I walked up the gang plank of the steamer to leave.

It seemed a long time before the Statue of Liberty appeared on the horizon. But when, at last, she came into view, I rapturously gazed upon her and soliloquized:

"If you ever gaze upon me again you will have to turn around. I have returned to the government that is performing services for its citizens. I can now understand that the cost of these services has not been met by geese that lay golden eggs, and that my taxes have not been one sided transfers of wealth. I shall willingly pay taxes for such services as were absent in Trinigonia, and my only objection will rise when public funds are used for the gain of particular individuals or communities."

Here the steamer bumped the landing. I thought I heard a woman's voice calling my name. I turned my head to hear more distinctly, and recognized my wife's voice calling, "Bill, get up and dress." And I did not even frown when she added, "Don't you know you have an appointment with your lawyer to make out your income tax return?"

PART III.   FARM INCOMES AND RURAL PROGRESS

(a)   Our Agricultural Income—By J. I. Falconer.

(b)   Farm Income and Standard of Life—By H. C. Taylor.

(c)   Factors Influencing Farmers Incomes—By John D. Black.

(d)   Relation of Income to Successful Farming—By O. G. Lloyd.

(e)   Relation of Standard of Life to Success in Farming—By E. L. Kirkpatrick.

OUR AGRICULTURAL INCOME*

J. I. FALCONER,

President of the American Farm Economics Association.

It seems to be the general opinion that the income of farmers is low when compared with the income to those engaged in other occupations or of other manners of living. True, it is difficult to evaluate and measure many of the elements going to make up the total income to agriculture or to compare this total with that of other occupations. Such statistical data as are available, however, tend to show a relative low income to the agricultural industry as a whole, and especially has this been true during the past few years, a period when to low income has been added a considerable depreciation to the capital value of the agricultural plant.

Perhaps the best evidence of the state of the comparative income to agriculture as contrasted with that of other occupations is to be found in the relative growth of population in the different groups. As has been pointed out, not only has the percent of rural population been decreasing, but the total number of people living on farms has actually decreased in number since 1910, last year alone to the amount of 649,000 persons, a decrease of 2 percent of the total number on farms at the beginning of the year. And this in the face of a constant increase in total population. For while in 1910 our farm population made up 35 percent of the total it now comprises only about 25 percent. It is apparent that many farmers and prospective farmers are leaving the farm because they feel that the opportunities of securing a satisfactory income are more promising in other lines of endeavor, and the fact that the movement continues would seem to add weight to the opinion.

In earlier years we have usually attributed the relatively low agricultural income to the abundance and ease with which new land and farm houses could be secured; to the rapid expansion of transportation facilities, and therefore the ease of expanding our agricultural production to a point where the supply for long periods of time when placed upon the market would not bring a price sufficient to net a satisfactory living and income to the producer. To the income from

*From Address at Tenth National Country Life Conference.

113

products was added an anticipated speculative income from rising land and property values, and in no small portion of cases the net wealth of the operator at time of death comprised only such gain as had been made through the rise in land values.

But this has been only one of the factors in increasing our agricultural output. There are others. We are sometimes prone to think of the industrial evolution as a thing which was completed back in the days when the steam engine or the loom was invented. That these were the days when the great progress was made in improving methods of production, that the date of the invention of the McCormick and Hussey reapers was the period when improved farm machinery was universally adopted. And yet I would venture to say that there was never a period in the history of our agriculture when the adoption of labor saving and cost reducing methods and practices was as universal in agriculture as during the past fifteen years. Mr. H. R. Tolley, of the United States Department of Agriculture, has shown that in agriculture the output per worker has doubled since 1870 and that in no period during that time was the rate of increase as rapid as in the years since 1910. Many instances and statistics could be quoted from nearly all phases of agriculture. In Greene County, Ohio, where it took 36 man hours to produce an acre of corn in the years from 1907-1911 it took only 25 hours in the years from 1922 to 1926. This is typical. The general adoption of the gas engine by farmers, a comparatively recent development, has worked revolutions. It is such progress which has made possible an increasing agricultural output with a decreasing farm population.

These improvements in the organization and methods of production are to be found not only in agriculture, but in industry, transportation, commerce, etc. We are experiencing a most remarkable advance in the productive efficiency of industry. Studies of the Bureau of Labor Statistics indicate, for example, that in the iron and steel industries in 1925 the output per worker was 50 percent greater than in 1914. In the automobile industry the output per man-hour was three times greater. In transportation the average amount of coal consumed in moving 1000 tons of freight and equipment one mile was 197 pounds in 1920. By 1925 this had been reduced to 156 pounds. Mass production, improved machinery, extended use of power and organized management are combining to increase in a remarkable manner the output of our mills and factories. There has been a general increase in the output per worker in the various occupations.

This increase in the productivity of labor in industry has been accompanied by increasing wages, increased purchasing ability and rising standards of living. True, the cost of living has risen also, but its advance has not been nearly as rapid as that of wages. The result is that the purchasing power of the typical wage earner has increased by nearly 30 percent since the pre-war days, and this is probably the explanation of the ability of the American people to continue to purchase in large amounts the things that pertain to a rapidly advancing standard of living.

Unfortunately for agriculture, however, this increasing ability to purchase on the part of our industrial population has largely gone towards expanding the demand for the products of industry rather than of agriculture. It has gone towards creating a demand for more and better automobiles, radios, houses, travel, etc., the desire for which is almost without limit. With agricultural products, however, the situation is different. The total demand for farm products in this country is relatively inelastic as far as total quantity is concerned. It is doubtful if the recent increase in the purchasing ability of our population has increased the demand for farm products to the extent that it has for other products. Much of the general increase in productive, and resulting increase in purchasing power has resulted in further demand for non-agricultural products. While with increasing output, agriculture has been left without a corresponding increase in the demand for its products. Thus bringing about an unfavorable ratio to the farmer between farm products sold and the supplies and necessities purchased.

Indeed, there is evidence to show that without increasing well being and substitution of machine for hand labor, that the consumption of farm products is less per capita rather than more. While some products have been increasing in per capita consumption others have been decreasing. Add to this; improvements in the technique of farm production have demanded an increased investment in capital good, largely, the product of industry and some of which like the automobile, truck and tractor have actually resulted in decreasing the demand for farm products. In Ohio for instance to have fed the horses which have been eliminated since 1910 would require today 10 percent of the crop area of the state. All of which has tended to expand the demand for the products of industry rather than of agriculture.

So far as quality in farm products is concerned the situation is different. Never has there been a more effective demand for quality in farm products than during the past few years, and those farmers who have been in a position to take advantage of this expanded demand for quality have been in the most favored position as regards income.

For the foregoing reasons among others it has been difficult for agriculture to secure a rightful share of the surplus which it has helped to create.

An adjustment, however, is going on in the way of a movement of producers from the farm to the city and a steady increase in consuming population, a movement which with time, providing the character of our population is maintained, should bring about conditions more favorable for agriculture in securing an equitable share in the social dividend. The extent of the movement will depend to no small extent upon the degree to which agriculture maintains a standard of living comparable with that of other groups of society. Meanwhile in determining our agricultural policy consideration should be given to these facts and conditions that agriculture may not be made to pay more than her fair share of the price of progress.

FARM INCOME AND STANDARD OF LIFE*

By H. C. Taylor,

The Institute of Land and Public Utility Economics, Northwestern University.

The starting point on which I want to center is about the things that Sir Horace Plunkett initiated when he sounded the note in the beginning days of this question of farm life by not ignoring the basic things that led up to it, but included in his rounded program better farming, better business, and better living. And I want to say to you today I believe the greatest of these is better living.

We have stressed greater efficiency in production and in marketing; we are now stressing better living. About twenty-five years ago I was in Washington in connection with some special work there and had the occasion to meet a labor leader. I remember with what astonishment I listened to this labor leader say, "Greater efficiency is not the thing we need now. What we need now is fairness in the distribution of the wealth, and it would be better if the total annual production of wealth in the United States were less and more equitably distributed." I was astonished, I say. I could not understand it. I was in the academic halls. I had not yet owned a farm. I had not yet traveled and visited large numbers of farmers. I had not felt the responsibility of leadership in the great bureau in Washington under the inspiration of the greatest Secretary of Agriculture, who felt that the department of agriculture is no use unless it serves the people. Today if one should make that statement with regard to labor it would be astonishing for the reason that labor has attained the purpose that leader was striving to attain and labor has secured what the leaders believed to be a fair share in the national income. But if some one should make that same remark today with regard to agriculture, namely, that what we want is not so much greater efficiency and it would be better today if the total annual income of the nation were somewhat less and we had a more equitable distribution of that wealth among those who participated in its production—I say if some one should make that statement today I should not be astonished, but impressed that nobody had made the statement.

*From Address at Tenth National Country Life Conference.

117

We come then to the question of how the farmer may secure a larger share of the national income, and in discussing this question I am approaching it today from the angle of the relation of the standard of living to the share of agriculture in the national income. I want us to continue teaching increased efficiency both in production and in marketing, but as I said in the beginning, we need to devote particular attention to the question of efficiency in living. I agree with what has been said with regard to the production of increased efficiency in agriculture being as a rule quickly distributed to other groups through cheaper food supplies.

I do not agree with what Dr. Black said with regard to the rapidity with which the products of increased efficiency in industry in the cities are diffused from those industries to other groups.

Within the last six months I have had occasion to be, not in close touch, but in touch with the economists of the Business Men's Commission on Agriculture. Considerable correspondence was carried on, because it was found by the economists that my testimony disagreed with the testimony of most of the people. The testimony, according to the claim, was that most of the people believed that increased efficiency would solve the problem. Here and there the farmers had been picked and came before the commission, who as individuals had been efficient, and, being very much more efficient than their neighbors, had a larger income. Naturally if one did not go into the matter far enough he may think that all farmers were as efficient as those particular farmers, and, of course, had as good an income as those particular farmers; and that farmers were not suffering.

But if all farmers were as efficient as those particular farmers and produced as much per acre as those particular farmers what would be true of the total surplus, and what would be true of the prices and what would be true of the profits of these particular people? In correspondence with this Business Men's Commission a letter finally came, after the exchange of many letters, in which it said, " It seems to be true that when increased efficiency is brought to pass in a particular city industry that city industry is very effective in holding the increased profits of the increased efficiency for the benefit of those who participate in the industry as stockholders or as workers, but it seems to be true that agricultural competition is so keen that increased efficiency as it spreads on larger and larger numbers is gradually and certainly diffused to the consumer and not held for the benefit of those who participate in the industry." I am very glad to have that letter in my files for future reference in case the report, when it comes out, ignores our correspondence.

The distribution of wealth comes about as a result of competition, and, in the first place, the distribution of wealth is the product of price relations. The price of what we sell and the price of what the other fellow sells determines the distribution of wealth as between different occupations. Supply and demand and competition are the forces that are supposed to determine price. Now the reason that certain occupation groups have larger incomes than other occupation groups is because there is keener competition in some groups than in other groups.

If any one should ask me, "What is the most characteristic and important trend in modern economic life in America today," I would answer it in this phrase, "Competition limited." The whole trend is toward the limitation of competition. The whole trend under the organized direction of government is to limit competition. Only the other day under the direction of the Federal Trade Commission a meeting was held on the Pacific Coast with several hundred representatives of the people, practically all the people participating, milk, butter, poultry, dairy products, all the people in these products represented, for the purpose of developing trade rules and practically all the people in that region agreed to these new trade rules. The idea is to put competition on a higher plane.

But read carefully the first resolution passed under the supervision of the Federal Trade Commission and you find that what it means is this: that one milk buyer or butter buyer will not compete with another milk buyer or butter buyer buying and trying to get the product of the other milk buyer's customers. If I am selling to one man, you are selling to the same man, and another man is buying butter or milk, or whatever product we are producing here as a trade agreement, so long as I have a contract with the one buyer the other buyer is not to approach me in any way to try to get my business. A very definite limitation of competition. Now don't misunderstand me. I don't mean to say that the greater limitation of competition is not a good thing. We have been gradually limiting competition since the days of robbery, since the days when we could not have private property because somebody was trying to take it; when you could not produce a crop more than you could protect with your gun because somebody would get it.

The gradual building up of institutions that put competition on a high plane is a splendid thing, and so far as the newer limitations of competition look toward greater efficiency, reduced cost in marketing, they are a good thing, if they don't, at the same time, influence the distribution of wealth as between buyer and seller, between the consumer and producers of farm products or other products. But the great difficulty is just this, and it was the point made in Mr. Graham's letter, to which I made reference. Professor Graham, being an economist of the United States Chamber of Commerce associated with the business men's commission indicated that we are having more and more limitation of competition in the city industry and less and less competition in agriculture. We are not having a proportionate increase in competition in the country industries.

Now it is from this point of view that I want to stress the major point that is in the book to which reference was made, and I don't propose to elaborate on this occasion. We need to improve the means of limiting competition among farmers. Farmers are the most unmerciful competitors of each other we can find in the whole industrial world, and so long as they are such competitors of each other it is a grave matter to secure a fair income for them.

Now as to the matter or method of limiting competition, farmers are very much scattered, but with cooperation the time can come that farmers may utilize trade rules. With this system of information, the outlook reports that Dr. Smith mentioned, much can be done undoubtedly to put farmers in a position where they can see with a clearer eye the things they need to know in order to direct their products along the right lines and not push too much in one line and then in the other, with low prices in this line and then in the other, in other words, wiser direction of production.

But we need still other limitations of competition, those that have been mentioned yesterday and today, those that come from fewer people being in agriculture. We need only enough people in agriculture.

There is one thing more you should mention before going to that method. It is the legislative method which is being used so very effectively, and which was better discussed last night than I could discuss it, the legislative method of limiting competition in certain groups without applying the same legislative method of limiting competition for the agricultural product and giving the agricultural product advantage in the home market, as manufactured goods are given the advantage in the home market, but that I don't want to go into.

My time is passing, and I want to get on to the major point I wanted to stress this morning, namely, the question of standard of living in the relation of income. I want to say in the first place th' standard of living was originally an economic concept. I want the sociologists to appreciate the economists have used it in a particular sense. If they want to use it in other senses, very well, let's not get confused.

The whole approach of this subject of standard of living, in the first place, was the approach of one studying the distribution of wealth and factors that determine the share received by the different classes in competition with each other. To what extent will standards of living set a limitation of competition, and that is the point of view that I want to impress this morning, that in so far as farmers will work for nothing and board themselves and put cheap food and raw material on the market at a price far below the price at which they can produce it and live as other people live and stay on the farm, contented to do so, farm prices will remain low and farm incomes relatively low compared to the incomes of other groups. But in so far as farmers as a class insist upon a standard of living which to them is as satisfactory as the standard of living they could secure in other industries (or if they cannot secure it will go into other industries; some of them cannot, but will see that their children have the opportunity); then I say in so far as farmers have set their mind on a higher standard and insist on as satisfactory living conditions as they could get in other industries and live up to it and will go into other industries if they cannot secure that in farming; then the income of the farmer as a class will be as satisfactory and the living conditions of the farmer as a class will be as satisfactory, as satisfying as the incomes and the lives of other people.

This, of course, is entirely out of harmony with an old proverb, an old proverb which is in the unwritten Bible. I mean the uncanonized bible, the bible that comes in between the old Holy Bible and this recent rural sociologist bible, a bible that really fits into the days of Ben Franklin, and, of course, so far as it was canonized it was canonized by Ben Franklin.

The proverb I wish to refer to is "You cannot eat your cake and keep it." That proverb was true in the pioneer days of self sufficing agriculture, when the well being of the farmer and his family depended upon the bushels of potatoes in the bin, the barrels of apples in the cellar, the number of ham shoulders and sides that were nicely smoked and hanging in the smokehouse, and the supplies of wheat and corn and other food supplies that were available, and the amount of wool and flax that might be available for making clothing in the self sufficing day. It was true that you cannot eat your cake and keep it. The more you had in storage for your winter supplies the better you were off. We have changed from that condition to a commercial agriculture. We are producing for the market. We are now exchanging our supplies for other things that we want. I want to say that we can get more in the long run by the modern system, and I am not decrying the passing from the old to the new, but at the present time and continually, just in so far as we continue to follow the old proverb and live parsimoniously in order to save and put ourselves in the position of a man I knew in Iowa County, Wisconsin (I came pretty nearly saying gentleman). He started in with nothing and came to own 1900 acres of land. At the age of seventy he was in the field cultivating beans. He was dressed in a manner that implied great poverty. I talked with him about his philosophy of life and the methods he used to accumulate his great fortune. He said, "It ain't how much you make but how much you save that counts." And he meant it, and followed it up.

I looked into the matter and the story sounds something like I heard yesterday. I found his son was a policeman in Madison. A few weeks later I was talking to a graduate student who was rooming in the same house I was rooming in at the time. The graduate professor had been a high school professor in Michigan and had come over to Wisconsin to get his Ph. D. There was a young woman who had been teaching in that school, of whom he thought a great deal. He was buying her a diamond ring. He had not saved enough money before coming to school, but what he had to go into debt before he got his Ph. D. He had a bunch of rings sent from Chicago to look over. There was one particular one he wanted very much because it was the same size diamond ring his fiancee's friend had. After a long struggle he bought it and said, "It is not what you save but what you use that you get the good out of." He got his Ph. D. He married the woman. I visited them in their home within the last year. He is a successful professor. He has not lacked the good things of life, and he is rendering an important social service.

This leads me, then, to say that we must change our proverb from "You cannot eat your cake and keep it," to the new one which I do not believe is in the rural sociologist's bible. I had a chance to put it in, but at that time I thought I must be rather dignified and didn't put it in, but I feel today I can do as I please. The new proverb is "You must eat your cake to keep it."

That, in simple language, is the simple truth that I have to bring to you today. When the product of increased efficiency, or the product of improved conditions, due to the withdrawing of certain legislation which is disadvantageous to the farmer, or bringing him legislation which puts him more nearly in a position of fairness with other groups, when that comes, if it is used in building up land values on the one hand or increased product on the other hand, thus reducing the prices of those products it is diffused to other classes and ceases to be available for consumption. It is only in so far as this larger income due to greater efficiency or fair legislation is used and built into the higher standard of living that you can hope to have it, and it becomes a factor of limiting competition of farmer with farmer. It is only in so far as it operates as a factor in limiting competition of farmer with farmer, that the farmer as a class will be able to hold that increased income as a continuous stream year after year.

So remember this. The old proverb of the day of Ben Franklin will have to be discarded. That is fundamentally of an order that we cannot accept. The new proverb is, "You must eat your cake to keep it."

FACTORS INFLUENCING FARMERS' INCOMES*

JOHN D. BLACK,

Professor of Agricultural Economics, The University of Minnesota

This question may be approached from two directions, that of factors affecting the income of farmers as a class, and that of factors affecting the relative incomes of different individual farmers. I shall consider the first of these only.

I realize that this subject calls merely for a proper application of the elementary principles of economics, and the restating of some commonplace economic maxims, and that it will therefore be very difficult to make it sound fresh and interesting.

To begin with, the income per agricultural worker in the United States depends a great deal upon how many such workers there are in proportion to the agricultural resources of the United States. Under agricultural resources should be included not only land and land improvements, but livestock, buildings and other equipment. Other things being the same, and in a given state of agricultural technique, the output per worker in agriculture decreases with the number of such workers per unit of land and farm capital. With no improvement in the arts of agricultural production, and except on the very frontier of agriculture, income per worker decreases as the number of workers increase. The United States had 11 agricultural workers per square mile of agricultural land in 1920; Denmark, 44; Japan, 503. Farm wages in the United States averaged $364 per year in 1913; in Denmark, $185; in Japan, less than $40. A further circumstance is that as the number of agricultural workers increases, also more and more of them resort to low-grade land.

The foregoing must not be taken to mean that incomes per worker are constantly declining. In the United States, at least, and probably in most of the world, the trend has generally been in the opposite direction. The supply of agricultural capital per worker, and the improvements in agricultural technique, have come faster than the population remaining on the land, with the result that incomes per farm worker have increased.

*From Address at Tenth National Country Life Conference.

123

But at the same time, urban production has also improved its technique and increased its quota of capital goods per worker, so that the per-worker incomes of city people have also increased faster than the population. A recent report from the Secretary of Commerce's office shows that the output per person engaged in manufacturing in the United States has increased 50 percent since 1899, and 40 percent even since 1919. I do not know which increase has been the faster, urban industry's or agriculture's.

Many things grow out of the comparative rate of increase in output per worker in city and country. If the city advances the more rapidly, farm people gain from lower relative prices for city-made goods—as they have gained from the constantly lower prices for city-made automobiles. If the farm advances the more rapidly, then city people gain from constantly cheaper food prices. But population movements also greatly affect the results. If farms gain rapidly in efficiency, and the number of agricultural workers does not decline, then farm products, due to their relatively inelastic demand, may fall so low in price that farm incomes may actually decline in money terms. Unless a parallel movement occurs in the city, then the real income of the farm people—that is, incomes in purchasing power—will also decline. A sudden or rapid increase in agricultural efficiency is seldom accompanied by a sufficient cityward movement of the population to keep real farm incomes from declining temporarily.

A sudden expansion of agriculture into new areas—as recently of cotton-growing into a western cotton frontier—may have the same effect as the foregoing.

In the long run, farmers probably share fully as much in increases in urban efficiency as city people do in increases in rural efficiency. Any one who observes thoughtfully one day in the life of a modern farm family will realize that city achievements have contributed more to putting it upon its present plane than have agricultural achievements. Yet there is one important off-setting circumstance—there is a growing class of people who produce nothing in the present and live on the interest and rent from wealth accumulated in the past by them or their forebears, who share in the improvements of civilization on the same basis as those who work, and most of such people live in the city. Few of the leisured class make their homes in the country. Increases in farm efficiency are clear boons to such. All that agriculture gets back is a problematical lowering of the interest rates.

The agricultural production of all countries affects the farm incomes in any one country. The richer the agricultural resources of a country, other things being the same, the larger the surplus of farm products it will put on the market to feed the urban population of its own and other countries. The same is true, up to a certain point, as the agricultural population of a country increases. The certain point mentioned is the point at which rural population becomes so dense that it begins to eat up the surplus. Densely populated areas such as in the Orient have very little agricultural surplus. If the agricultural resources of a country or region are inferior, it either must have a relatively extensive agriculture, which means a relatively small agriculture, or else a very low level of income for its agricultural people. Denmark, with poor agricultural resources, has chosen the former. Her agriculture, next to England's is the most extensive in Europe. Italy, also with poor resources, has chosen the latter. Erecting tariff barriers to protect agriculture under such circumstances, as Italy has done, will make agriculture more intensive than it otherwise would be, and increase the number of agricultural workers, but it will not, except at the beginning of such a policy, ordinarily raise the level of real farm incomes. Farm wages are twice as high in Denmark as in Italy.

Large agricultural resources per agricultural worker means extensive agriculture—a large amount of land or capital goods or both per worker. It also means doing a large part of the work with machinery, except on purely livestock farms or ranches.

It also ordinarily means large farms, if not as measured in acres, at least as measured in output.

There may be, however, as in eastern Germany, large farms and yet low incomes per worker. This is because most of the workers are farm laborers.

This leads to the important consideration that if incomes per worker are to really high, the workers must themselves own considerable land and capital goods. Having a large amount of land and capital goods to work with increases the income of a worker somewhat even if the worker has to pay rent or interest for the use of them; but nowhere nearly so much as when he owns them himself. The proportion of farm wealth which is owned by landlords and covered by mortgages and notes greatly affects the incomes of the actual workers.

Some look upon a high agricultural birth-rate as lowering incomes per agricultural worker. It does this only in case not enough of the sons and daughters go to the city; and probably this has usually been the condition in most of the western world ever since the industrial revolution came on. There is almost always a lag in the city-ward flow of the farm population. A tremendous amount of economic pressure is needed in the aggregate to get ten to fifteen million young men and women each generation to break home ties and seek fortunes in strange cities; and the higher the rural birth-rate, probably the greater the lag. Our rural people of European origin have generally had large families in the first generation, and their sons and daughters have been much more inclined to remain in agriculture. The country-side is patched with areas largely peopled with the sons and daughters of small groups of foreign folks who settled down in the centers of them a few generations ago. The little Swiss settlement in Green County, Wisconsin, is now overflowing the boundaries of that county. It has been observed frequently that farms are smaller, agriculture more intensive, wages lower and land values higher in such areas than in otherwise similar areas roundabout. The balance of population between rural and urban in the United States has been greatly affected in the past by such circumstances as the foregoing.

Immigration has affected the situation in still another way. Mere numbers of workers in proportion to agricultural resources does not alone tell the whole story. It depends, in addition to several things already mentioned, upon how hard they work. One fifth more hours of work per day, provided the rate of work is not slackened, is nearly the same as having one-fifth more workers. It is all right to have a fifth more work provided it doesn't give agriculture over-production at the time. Although it is easy to exaggerate the industry of our farm peo-ple—in many sections there is not much farm work to do for a con-siderable part of the year—nevertheless it is probable that they have worked harder in the aggregate than most other occupational groups in the same region. This applies perhaps even more to the farm women than to the farm men. There are two major reasons for this, one, the European sense of relative worth of income as measured against the disutility of work that our rural immigrant classes brought with them; and second, a similar heritage of relative values that has been carried down from pioneer days or at least from the straitened days of their cwn boyhood on the farm.

Let it not be understood at this point that I am arguing for "re-striction of output" per worker, which labor unions have sometimes practiced. The point is that if farm people are going to work a fifth harder than other folks, then at the same time we must have fewer of them.

Their working harder than other folks, however, is probably not so significant as their denying themselves more comforts and luxuries and saving harder—at least until recently. As the result of this they have, it is true, accumulated more land and equipment to work with; but unfortunately as things now work out, no sooner is it accumulated than all or part of it is carried off to the city by the retiring farmer, or by the heirs who have chosen their lot in the city. If American agriculture could only have retained all the wealth that it has produced and saved in the last century, much of our country-side would now look like a gorgeous succession of country estates. Part of the resources accumulated by hard savings has also regularly gone into the market to increase the demand for land and bid up its price.

Let it be understood that I am not suggesting less saving, but rather that more present income go into rural betterments—into better farm buildings, better homes, into durable consumption goods, better health, better schools and education, better roads. These are all ways of saving up for the future that mean more for agricultural people than larger fortunes to pass on to the city.

There is much to be said for the sense of social justice of a certain farmer I once knew. He said to his two sons. "All I've got is in this farm here. I'll send either of you boys that wants to go to the city and give you a city man's education—lawyer, doctor, preacher, anything you want. But the other feller gets the farm when I'm through. We'll have to mortgage the farm to put one of you through college; but the rest of us will wipe that out in the next five or ten years." It is of interest that when the proposition was put on this basis, both wanted the farm.

Neither let me be misunderstood as thinking of income solely in money terms. A large part of the real values in living, and especially in rural living, come from the home life and the pleasures and satisfactions created within the family circle, from the family garden, from the satisfactions associated with work on the farm and watching and helping things grow, from the special delights of readily available rural types of recreation and sociability. I am inclined to believe that perhaps half or a third of the real values possible in rural living are attainable in spite of what you and I would surely call a small money income.

It is plain from the foregoing that the whole problem of agricultural income brings itself to a head into a conventional economic equation of numbers of workers on the one hand, and how efficient they are and how hard they are willing to work and save, and the amount and quality of the other production elements they have to work with, and on the other hand, of the consuming power and disposition of the world population relative to farm products. But it is also made clear that back of even the number of workers, and back of the hours and the saving and all the rest, are customs and practices and social arrangements and traditional points of view and senses of relative values which constitute most of the real explanation of income. Included in the social arrangements are such institutions as private property in land, and systems of land tenure and ways of inheriting land and other property. Change any of these and the supply situation may be profoundly affected. There are also some strictly legislative arrangements that affect the situation. The most important of these relate to taxation. Our protective tariff system also produces its effect. I belong to that school of thinkers who believe that government has done and can do much that affects the relative incomes of different social groups. Time does not permit the developing of this phase of the subject in more detail.

The farmer of the United States stands almost at the pinnacle of success in achieving high incomes. Only in a few regions still newer than our own is there any likelihood that farm incomes are higher. There is not the slightest chance that the people on American farms are sinking to that awful hell of European peasanthood that our politicians and gloom painters have portrayed. But there is always with us the question whether farm people are sharing equally with city people in the gains in income. It seems quite plain that they have not since 1919. The official figures show agricultural workers one-fifth under 1919 in real income, and city workers nearly as much above 1919. The profit-takers have undoubtedly gained more than urban labor. At the same time, in the rapid rise and fall of land values since 1916, and accompanying rapid turnover of farms, there has been a great reduction in the agricultural workers ownership of wealth. Landlords and mortgage holders owned 57 per cent of the farm wealth of Minnesota in 1925 as contrasted with only 51 per cent in 1920. The real equity of Minnesota farmers in their farms was less in 1925 than in 1910. Mortgages are being paid off very slowly at present. Here is a situation that calls for vigorous treatment. Unless the present generation of farmers pays off its mortgages before it passes on, we will see an alarming growth in mortgage indebtedness and tenancy.

The way of relief suggested by the foregoing is a pronounced extensification of agriculture, especially in terms of labor, larger farms and larger fields, larger herds of swine and cattle, more machinery and power and less hand labor. The trend in this direction is definitely under way. It should become stronger. You object that larger farms means more mortgages and tenacy. It does. It is working out that way at this moment. But this cannot be helped. It is only for the time being. The larger profits obtained from the larger operations will presently begin to wipe out the mortgages.

I know that among the country life workers in front of me are many who have a sneaking fondness for small farms and closely grouped neighborhoods. I can only say that they are not for this country of ours. Measured in terms of output, the size of farms in this country, so far as I can see, will never decrease. Measured in acres, they may do so easily, when world conditions change so that the trend is toward intensification again. Rural sociologists, if they wish to be helpful, should begin at once to readjust their thinking along the lines of social organization for an agriculture of large dimensions per farm family.

The problem of agricultural relief is a problem for the whole country taken as a unit. Nowhere are the incomes altogether adequate. Everywhere the mortgage situation is at least a little pressing. But in a much more important way, it is a regional problem. If corn fields need to become larger in Iowa, think how much more the cotton fields of Alabama need to become larger. In fact, it is doubtful if considerable of the Old South can afford to grow cotton at all. Some system of agriculture much more extensive must take its place if incomes are ever to be adequate. The situation is only a little less pressing in the hill regions of the Northeast, and the sandlands of Michigan and Wisconsin.

The most important obligation of the federal government in this connection is to facilitate the necessary shifting of land to less extensive uses,—especially to forestry and to grazing; and also facilitate the shifting of population that must accompany it. Its most important opportunity along this line is to make fuller use of its taxing power, partly to relieve the burdens of the regions most seriously affected, partly to stimulate the new developments needed. To illustrate, it might relieve the situation in some of the hill regions of the East by buying land and turning it into forest reserve and then in some way recompensing the local government units affected for their loss of revenue.

Of course in time most of the necessary adjustments will be made. The situation as between industry and agriculture will eventually become more stable. But should it be necessary for us to wait all this time when there are helpful things that real statemanship in office could give us?

RELATION OF INCOME TO SUCCESSFUL FARMING—THE MASTER FARMER*

O. G. LLOYD

Purdue University
Professor Rural Economics, Purdue University

Little more can be done in this paper than to present the problem and suggest one or two solutions which it is hoped will provoke constructive suggestions.

The relation of money income to successful farming as embodied in the Master Farmer accounts for about one-third of the points in his score card. To enable him to fully qualify in good home life and good citizenship money is necessary to build and equip a modern home, a graded school, a magnetic church and an adequate hospital. Such institutions are necessary or by definition Master Farmers and successful farming are not a reality.

The amount of money income on farms in the first instance affects marginal farmers more than Master Farmers. That farmers as a class are affected is shown by the situation in the last seven years with city wages more than 50 per cent higher than the index number of farm prices.[1] The money advantage of city over country is reflected in the returns per farmer for his labor and management equaling less than half of the earnings of workers in other occupations for these seven lean farm years 1920-26.[2] As a result agriculture's capital, earning 3 per cent, has declined from eighty to sixty billions of dollars and other business has earned 10 to 12 per cent and increased from ninety-eight to one hundred thirty billions of dollars.

Evidence that farmers are yielding ground in this economic struggle and are moving to the city in the hope of making higher money incomes is shown by the increase in the number of farm bankruptcies and the decrease in farm population. Farm bankruptcies equal more than 15 per cent of total bankruptcies, compared to six per cent the previous decade.[3] The decrease in farm population is nearly three

*Address at Tenth National Country Life Conference.
1 The Agricultural Situation Vol. 11, No. 7.
2 Compiled from National Industrial Conference Board Report and reports from the National Bureau of Economic Research and the Bureau of Agricutural Economics.
3 H. C. Taylor, The Journal of Land and Public Utility Economics, Vol. III, No. 2.

and three-fourths million.[4] This amounts to 11.2 per cent decrease in seven years and is eight times the percentage loss in the previous decade.

This shift in the farm population appears necessary for man labor on farms increased in productive efficiency approximately 11 per cent during the last decade. This permitted more acres per man and higher yields per acre and resulted in a larger total production although thirty-one million less acres of farm land were in use than in the five years previous.

These shifts in income and population from farms to cities change the share of agriculture in the current income of the people of the United States from more than 20 per cent in the previous decade to less than 10 per cent[5] these last seven lean years 1920-26. While the wealth per capita of the farm population decreased nearly one-fourth since 1920 the wealth per capita of the remaining population increased nearly one-third.[6]

On this dwindling base of wealth per capita lies the foundation to support rural institutions which should compare favorably with those in the city. Such adequate homes, schools, churches, hospitals are necessary to hold Master Farmers on the land and these institutions require money.

Most farmers get more satisfaction in feeding hogs or cows if they pay. Out of 800 Iowa farmers questioned, all except a few stated they would live in the city if they believed they could make more money there.

Farmers with the least property and the least responsibility in times of agricultural depression go to the cities first and the largest property owners go last.[7] The poorest farmers are eliminated first and some successful farmers choose the city believing it offers greater opportunities.

Let us admit that more and more rural people will compare their opportunities with urban people and demand equal facilities. On the other hand it does not follow that rural-minded people will not accept a smaller money income and less conveniences to live on the farm than in the city, while the urban minded dweller will accept less money and fewer conveniences to live in the city.

It is in this sense that two civilizations exist side by side—the rural-minded which will persist in the country by choice regardless

4 Yearbook of Agriculture 1926, pp 1,235 and Crops and Markets, May 1927, pp 187.
5 Henry C. Taylor, op. cit.
6 Compiled from National Industrial Conference Board Report and from National Bureau ofEconomic Research.
7 Movement of Population, Cornell Bulletin 426, by Dr. E. C. Young.

of lower money incomes than could be obtained in the city and the urban-minded which will persist in the city notwithstanding possibilities of a higher income on the farm.

It is a fact, according to Dr. W. I. King, that there have not been any wholesale migrations from country to city. This is evidence that before the irreducible minimum money income is reached, which is necessary to maintain the standard of living of Master Farmers, that farm money incomes increase.

Such agricultural depressions as the present one correct themselves in time. Such valleys of depressions will probably be followed by peaks of agricultural prosperity. These wide swings of the pendulum of agriculture create unstable conditions which result in high long-time average prices to consumers and low low-time average returns to farmers.

That standards of living rise with higher farm incomes is shown by Dr. Eben Mumford's Michigan studies covering 1,000 farms. Other studies such as Dr. E. L. Kirkpatrick's lead us to the same conclusion. What constructive measures will promote higher money incomes on farms and more adequate rural institutions?

First, an agricultural education which teaches rural people how to play and work together. This should begin in the public schools and continue through the high schools and colleges. Text books and teachers should have the rural point of view. At present a critical examination would show that text books used in Vocational Agriculture and Agricultural Colleges are largely, if not entirely, written by those who live in cities, think in terms of city ways and write as they live and think.

School teachers are trained in the city by Professors who live in the city. These school teachers naturally imitate the thinking, the prejudices and the preferences of their urban Professors who determine what the students' grades shall be and when they are prepared to graduate.

The content of courses in such rural-minded schools as proposed would teach group action. Part of the requirements of a course would be membership in an organization which would teach the value of group control. Its responsibilities as well as its opportunities would be emphasized.

Such training in community cooperation would make state and national cooperation successful. This would enable a production program to succeed which would largely stabilize agriculture and benefit consumers as well as farmers. Denmark's success lies in her Folk Schools. Denmark is profiting now from teaching a generation of boys and girls the lessons of cooperation and has emphasized well-balanced production as essential in profitable marketing.

Without a production-price consciousness, a stable agriculture is improbable; without stability agriculture is not worth being called a business; if not business-like, agriculture will yield insufficient money income to challenge the best rural manhood—the source of Master Farmers.

Second, a taxation plan should be promoted which more nearly rests on the group receiving the benefits and having the ability to pay.

The economy of division of labor and the application of the law of diminishing returns affect the distribution of wealth and are related to taxation policy.

The economy in the division of labor continues to make it increasingly necessary for farmers to specialize. More and more, farmers will limit their work to the production of the raw materials which will be processed off the farm. This economy in specialization is one of the principal reasons for the decrease in farm population. The increased productive efficiency of the farmer now enables him to produce for his family and that of three other families. This is largely due to spinning, weaving, tanning, making shoes, butchering and butter-making being done now in the city where it can be done more cheaply.

The law of diminishing returns per acre or per square mile becomes operative sooner in farming than in other occupations. After about four cultivations of corn it is likely more profitable to work other land, for the increased yield due to the fifth plowing may not pay for the cost of labor involved. In most other businesses large investments of capital and correspondingly large incomes can be derived from a small area and increasing returns are obtained with the increased concentration of business on the same area.

For this reason the same agricultural area cannot give as much money support to its institutions as urban business. Again many businesses located in cities get all their support from the country. For instance, grain elevators, mail order houses, and packing houses located in cities pay city taxes and are supported largely from the country. The country continues to feed the city with a substantial part of its population, born and trained in the country. From 1920 to 1927 this cityward population was more than 11 per cent of the farm population. The city should help support the institutions that train cityward persons up to the time they go to the city. The general property tax falls most heavily on those with tangible property—the farmers. This tax is inequitable and should be supplemented by income, sales and other taxes which will bear more heavily on urban dwellers.

Without taxes levied according to benefits derived and ability to pay, rural institutions cannot receive the money support necessary to have them compare favorably with urban institutions serving the same purpose.

A Master Farmer is a *good husband and father.* This requires[8]

1. Convenient house.
2. Labor saving equipment in home.
3. Education and training of children.

He must be a good citizen—

1. Be a good neighbor.
2. Interest in school and churches.
3. Interest in other community enterprises.
4. Interest in local, state and national governments.

The general farm appearance and upkeep, and the equipment and operation of the farm are part of the score card. All these require money and time. Both leisure time and money income, comparable to that obtained in the city for the use of equal capital, labor, and management are essential to retain the Master Farmer on the land.

Such leisure time and such a money income obtainable on the farm are largely dependent on—

1. A more stabilized agriculture. This will largely eliminate agricultural crises like the present one.
2. Such leisure time and such a money income are dependent upon a more just system of taxation.

Such a long-time program will help insure the money income necessary to keep the Master Farmer on the land, and thereby render a service to all economic groups.

8 The Prairie Farmer's Score Card for Farmers, Vol. 97, No. 25.

THE RELATION OF THE STANDARD OF LIFE TO SUCCESS IN FARMING*

E. L. KIRKPATRICK

Associate Agricultural Economist, U. S. Department of Agriculture

Efforts to discover the existing relations between a standard of life and successful farming call at once for definition and clarification of the terms with which we are dealing. On the one hand, standard of life must be distinguished from standard of living and level of living. On the other hand, success in farming must be visualized in some term more inclusive than labor income or farm income, that is, financial returns from farming.

SUCCESS IN FARMING: During the past two decades considerable progress has been made in comparing the profitableness of farming, in terms of income and rate of returns on capital invested, with profitableness of other occupations and industries. It is desirable that these comparisons be continued and that additional and more precise measures of profitableness of farming be developed as rapidly as possible. Extreme caution must be used, however, that profitableness is not accepted by the public, by farm people especially, to mean success in farming. Briefly, success in farming involves more than income, as used ordinarily, more than "financial turnover" of an enterprise or a business. Success in farming does not lie in the ability to pile up wealth; in the form of cash, credit, lands or live stock, although this may be a contributing factor. Nor is success in farming co-ordinate with the number of sons and daughters who choose to follow the occupation of farming although this may be another contributing factor. What then is success in farming? What tangible and intangible factors does it embody?

In the words of Dr. Bailey, success in farming is the ability to make a full and comfortable living from the land, to rear a family carefully and well, to be of service to the community and to leave the farm more productive than it was when he (the farmer) took it. Viewed in this light success in farming becomes the embodiment of the satisfactions which the farm family finds in its calling and its sur-

*Address at Tenth National Country Life Conference.

135

roundings. Sources of these satisfactions are the tangible goods furnished by the farm for family living purposes, the financial returns from farming—cash or credit—entitling the farm family to draw upon the community's supply of consumption goods not available from individual family effort, and the intangible factors, inherent in no other occupation as in farming. A well-organized and operated farm is virtually a cooperative organization on a small scale; it involves the cooperation of all members of the family as does no other occupation or business. It creates a social and a business atmosphere which no other enterprise creates or permits. It carries a feeling of security of ownership which tends to develop a state of mind in harmony with an environment where individuals normally live at their best. These and other intangible factors "bulk large" in the satisfactions to be had from farming.

Success in farming may be regarded, then, as the index of satisfactions or values accruing to the family from the occupation of farming and from living in the farming community. These satisfactions or values are largely immeasurable.

STANDARD OF LIFE: At present the cost of living (value of goods used) bids fair to become the accepted measure of the level of living and the standard of living among farmers. While fairly applicable in this respect the cost of living will not serve as a measure of the satisfactions or values constituting family life, any more than "financial turnover" will suffice as a measure of success in farming. The cost of living is merely a measure of the variety, quantity and quality of goods used for family living purposes. Family life is the sum total of values evolving from the acquisition and use of goods and the use of time in the satisfaction of human wants. These values are intangible. They vary with the temperament, the capacities and the social relationships of the individual (or individuals composing the family). The standard of life is the sum total of these intangible values conceived as possible from the acquisition and use of goods and the use of time in the fulfillment of human wants. Made up of intangible values for which, as yet, no satisfactory method of measurement has been found the standard of life is immeasurable. But the goods, facilities and services, from the acquisition and the use of which the bulk of these values are attained are measurable. And the variety, quality and quantity of these goods held necessary to provide specific satisfactions or values in life, constitute the standard of living. The standard of (family) living, then, is the family's conception of the economic goods required to meet the physical and psychic needs of the different individuals composing the family.

The level of living is the variety, quantity and quality of economic goods actually consumed during a given period of time, a year, by the family (or group of families, on the average) regardless of whether these goods are sufficient to meet the physical and the psychic needs and wants of the different members of the family. While the standard of living represents the array of goods regarded essential to provide the quality of life desired the level of living designates the extent to which the needs and wants of the family are met.

In most farming communities success in farming is interpreted in terms of the standard of life sought and the quality of life attained by the farm family, rather than by the financial returns or the wealth accumulated from farming. This is illustrated by a comparison of two farm families as described by a farm economist, formerly a county superintendent of schools, as follows:

Mr. A. and Mr. X were both farmers living in the Willow Grove school community. Mr. A was said to be the best farmer although it was conceded by all the neighbors of both that Mr. X. was making the most money and holding the best farm in the community. I made the acquaintance of these two farmers and their families at my first opportunity. I wanted to know something of their farms and to learn why Mr. A. was regarded as the best farmer when it was conceded that Mr. X held the best farm.

Although not adjoining, the two farms were similar. Each contained 160 acres of tillable land of about the same topography and the same degree of fertility.

At the time of my first visit Mr. A had been owner and operator of his farm for six years during which time he had made minor improvements about the farmstead. The farmhouse of some forty years had been repainted and substantial fences had been placed around the farm orchard and garden.

"We bought the place for a home," said Mr. A, "and we came over here from White Oak to be near a good school and a live church and to get into a better community. We had to get the children nearer to school. We have five and the third will start to school this fall. They must have the school, they need the church and they will enjoy the social life of the community."

"This makes a satisfactory home for your family, then," I inquired.

"Just now it does," replied Mrs. A, "but we'll need to improve it and fix it up as we go along. The children will need more room and better things in the house as they get older. We came here with the hope of being able to enjoy a comfortable farm home, school the children and share the social, religious and civic life of the community. In the six years we have the farm partially paid for. Presently, we will be able to give more attention to the children."

"You'll soon need some more land," I remarked, "with the five children, four of them boys, coming on."

"That will be for the children to help decide when they are older," remarked Mrs. A. "If in the future they prefer more land to farm instead of better home life and an education then they may get it, but that is a good ways off. Now, we have land enough to keep us all busy, and yet we find time for some leisure and recreation, as we go along."

Calling upon family X several days later after visiting family A, I learned that Mr. X had owned and operated his farm of 160 acres for 10 years during which time he had "tiled out" each field, built new barns and rebuilt the farm house. Both barns and house were modern for the period represented, about a generation ago. "I came over here from Aspen to *own a good farm* and folks will tell you I've got it," said Mr. X. "None better in the county, I guess."

"Do you find good schools and things of that sort here?" I asked.

"The schools ought to be good considerin' the taxes I pay. I don't plan to put 'em through school anyway. The boys have more schooling now than I ever got and if they want any more they'll get it of their own accord without my help. She (referring to his wife) plans to put the girl through school and send her on to college; but that's their affair."

"But isn't it probable that in the future men will need more schooling to get on as well as you have," I asked. "Depends on the men and what they go into," replied Mr. X. "I'm fitting 'em out for farmers and it's no use to waste tim and money on schooling.'"

"And your church," I reminded, "you find a church of your liking here, I suppose?"

"Well, we still go over to Aspen when the weather and the roads are fit. When the weather's bad they (the children) go up here. I don't know much about their church up here but at any rate it's only Sunday School."

Careful study from all angles for the decade following revealed to me clearly the equality of life prevailing in each of the two homes. In home A the farmer and his wife were happily engaged in sharing life, work, play, worship and ideals with their children. I knew Mr. A to spend hours reasoning with his boys as to the best adjustment of cultivators, the handiest ways of breaking colts or the most suitable plan of crop rotation. At the request of Mr. A and Mrs. A, I spent many an evening at their home discussing different lines of work and relating my college experiences as best I could in order that the children might develop a genuine desire for a college education.

"We want the children to know something of the outside world and of life," was the common expression of either Mr. or Mrs. A. "Then, if they want to farm they ought to make good farmers and better citizens of the communities in which they live."

Driving down the road toward the A farm one day I was surprised to see a new addition to the farm house well under construction. "Yes," I was informed, on arrival at the farm, "we decided to enlarge and fix up the house while we are all here to use it. The children will never enjoy it more than now. They are growing up, you know."

Two years later a modern home surrounded with attractive plantings adorned the farmstead.

In home X, Mr. and Mrs. X seldom shared the work or play or discussed the ideals or the objectives of family life with their children. Here, things went on with regularity; time to get up, time to chore and time to get to the field. Mr. X's farm hands including the boys were first in the community to get out in the mornings and the first to pull in evenings. But the longer evenings after supper were usually spent in "prolonged choring," looking after fences, cutting weeds from the pasture, working in the garden, greasing the wagons and storing the machinery. So far as I know, the family never spent an evening playing games, singing or telling stories together. Quite true, the piano was played and books and papers were often read but free and wholesome family fellowship was lacking.

While Mr. and Mrs. A enlarged, remodeled and refurnished their house to maintain a satisfactory home life, Mr. X bought two additional farms, one of them in Canada, because he considered them good investments.

Recently I took occasion to trace the children of these two families. . Of the four sons of Family A, three had attended and graduated from the state agricultural college. The fourth was at that time attending a secular college and had made a splendid record in music. The daughter spent two years at this same college before marrying a farm boy in the home community. Of the three boys who attended the state agricultural college, two are farming, (one on the home farm) in the home community and the other is a successful county agricultural agent. The two sons and the daughter living on farms are all leaders in the civic and social life of the community.

Of the two sons of family X, neither finished high school. One became a garage mechanic and the other after taking a business course became a clerk in a village bank. The daughter while attempting to work her way through college stopped to teach school and at the end of her first year's teaching became the wife of a village restaurant keeper.

Having traced the children of these two families I am no longer in doubt as to why Mr. A was regarded as the best farmer although Mr. X held the best farm.

Thus it is noted that family A was concerned with the attainment of the highest possible satisfactions or values from the acquisition and use of goods and from the occupation of farming with its environment. Concerned chiefly with the realization of a high standard of family life, farmer A was recognized as the most successful farmer in the community. Concerned chiefly with the accumulation of wealth, rather than with the realization of a high standard of life farmer X appears to have missed many of the satisfactions which normally accrue from the occupation of farming, with its environment.

It is hoped that the foregoing presentations have indicated that economic returns do not constitute a complete measure of success in farming and that goods, facilities and services used are not always indicative of the satisfactions or values enjoyed by the family. When interpreted in their broader meaning a standard of life and success in farming are both essential parts of the same process; that is, success in farming is the realization of a high standard of family life. The economic aspects of both play a major part. Larger economic returns will not improve the quality of family life if rational desires and ideals are lacking.

But it must be recognized that the two families described above were moderately prosperous farm families in a prosperous farming community. Financial returns were sufficient to make possible the attainment of a high standard of family life by either family. There are many less prosperous farming communities where meagre financial returns with many families appear to be the limiting factors in the attainment of a high standard of life. Goods, facilities and services necessary to provide the major satisfactions of life are not available. It is to communities of this type that attention and study must be given in order to determine quantitatively the extent to which a prevailing standard of life is reflected in success in farming.

PART IV. THE AMERICAN COUNTRY LIFE ASSOCIATION AFTER TEN YEARS

(a) The Country Life Movement—By K. L. Butterfield.

(b) An Interpretation of the Lansing Conference—By A. R. Mann.

(c) Past Issues and Future Hopes—By Carl C. Taylor.

(d) Officers and Committees—By Nat T. Frame.

THE AMERICAN COUNTRY LIFE MOVEMENT*

KENYON L. BUTTERFIELD

There are two approaches to the discussion of a "movement": we may describe things that are being done, or we may attempt to indicate the ideas underlying such efforts.

In American country life there is no movement in the sense of a closely knit organized endeavor, with central power-stations commanding many units of effort. There is a multitude of separate enterprises and improvements. School, farmers' organization, church, each has its own program of progress more or less well developed. But there is no one comprehensive all-inclusive organized program that seeks to incorporate all these plans into some unified scheme of activity.

But there are, I believe, certain big ideas back of all these efforts. Some of these ideas are clear cut, some are just developing and are yet to be made a real force. The more important of these ideas I want to discuss as an essential part of what we may fairly call the American Country Life Movement.

First of all, what is the "country-life field"? Let me recall to your minds the scope of the American Country Life Association:

1. Rural home life
2. Rural education
3. Morals and religion
4. Rural government
5. Rural health and sanitation
6. Rural recreation and social life
7. Rural charities and corrections (or rural social work)
8. Communication and transportation
9. Country planning
10. International rural interests
11. Cummunity development and organization
12. In general, how secure a "satisfying country-life" and how maintain or increase the quality of rural people?

Now all the parts of this dozen areas of work are interrelated, bound

* (President's Address, Eleventh Conference American Country Life Association, Urbana, Illinois, June 19, 1928.)

together most intimately.   Yet each topic means some important object for improvement, some worthy field of rural endeavor.

But I said that we were to discuss tonight not so much activities as the ideas back of those activities.   It seems to me that the American Country Life Movement recognizes at least the following important necessities in maintaining the quality of people on the land, which is after all the great inclusive end of rural progress:

1.   The necessity of a good economic foundation for a satisfying country life.   No man can tell just what is a fair reward for farming, nor how it can be obtained, but it is clear that reasonable economic prosperity for the great masses of the farmers is essential if we are to have a good type of life.

2.   Under modern conditions, it is urban industry that makes the market for the farmers, and this demand for food and other soil-grown products is the chief economic force in agricultural and country life development.

3.   The efficiency of the farmer is indispensable—good farming on good land.   Poor farming on poor land can hardly expect high reward.

4.   Farmers do live apart and cannot completely project the city into the country, even if they so desire, although the city apparently influences the country with respact to all sorts of standards of living and of life.   Modern transportation has transformed rural contacts. At the same time the mere fact of physical residence on separate farms and in small villages is bound to have a permanent influence on all rural questions.

These things, I say, the American Country Life Movement recognizes as fundamental and as constantly playing into the whole question of rural development from the standpoint of all aspects of organized procedure.

On the other hand, the Country Life Movement insists upon such principles of rural progress as the following:

1.   The countryside needs high grade social institutions adapted to the country and properly financed: the school, local government, economic organization, facilities for health and recreation, and religious organization,—must be in their way and for their purpose quite as effective as similar agencies in the city.   They require well-trained specialists just as in the case in the city.

2.   Continuing Education is indispensible in the country, as it is in the city.   When a youth leaves school, no matter what his age, he should find both a means and an incentive to keep on with his systematic education, through reading and study as well as through observa-

tion, as a continuing process all through life.

3.   Urban interests of themselves demand that the city shall pay attention to rural needs, and not only pay attention but help pay the taxes that shall furnish an adequate social structure to meet rural needs.

4.   Agricultural and rural needs should have a preferred position in all statesmanlike programs worthy of private or public origin.

5.   Well rounded Christian character demands that a farmer should obtain true happiness and growth whether in adversity or prosperity, out of life on the farm.   Here is a fundamental chance for the church.

6.   The local community is the most significant unit of rural organization.   We need programs for the counties, areas, states, regions, the nation, and the world; but in actual practice the local group is the most effective unit of endeavor.

Are there practical steps that we may contemplate at this time with some confidence, assuming that the opinions laid down thus far in this paper are reasonably sound?   Yes, many.   I should like to propose one especially that I think is the most important of any that could be suggested, namely, that an effort be made to forward more rapidly and more inclusively the community program movement in the United States in rural areas, and that we link up with some similar movements in other countries, like the International Country Life Commission and organizations for rural missions the world over.

I should like to see the extension forces, rural schools, rural churches, farmers' organization, together with many other agencies both in country and city, deliberately contemplate and plan a well defined rural project in the form of building and developing rural communities.

AN INTERPRETATION OF THE TENTH NATIONAL COUNTRY LIFE CONFERENCE

A. R. MANN

Dean of the New York State College of Agriculture

The purpose of this final expression is to gather up the ideas or concepts which have stood out as of chief importance from the standpoint of those who participated. It is no part of the speaker's task to modify these ideas by the injection of his own personal interpretation of them.

What, then, are some of the significant achievements and viewpoints resulting from this convention?

1. First, this conference has recognized the inter-national implications of its program and of the great issue of farm income and farm life. Its sessions have been dignified by the presence of many distinguished foreign visitors.

2. Farmers and farm women themselves have taken an active and influential part in its discussions. Qualified farmers have spoken, and they have made invaluable contributions.

The discussions here have revealed that farmers and so-called professional workers approach the problems in hand from different standpoints and in different attitudes of mind. A superficial impression may be gained that these two attitudes are irreconcilable. They are not. We must first learn to speak the same language, then we shall have the means of reaching common ground and uniting our efforts. Farmers have much to give to professional workers; they also have much to learn from such workers.

3. This conference has made a useful contribution in interlocking the two aspects of its theme, the economic and the social, farm income and farm life. Hitherto these have all too commonly been treated as separate things. In the conference book, in the addresses and the discussions, these two have merged into a common concept, the standard of life in the country and the means for its realization. I predict that there has been advanced here a singleness of objective, a wholeness in the conception of life, which will come in time to have marked in-

146

fluence on both economics and sociology as fields of inquiry, and in personal and community programs of action.

The starting point has been a recognition of both longtime trends and the severe agricultural depression of recent years and the distress which it has produced; of the growing numerical disproportion between rural and urban populations; the disparity between farm prices and industrial prices; between the 70% non-farming population enjoying 92% of the national income and the 30% farm population not enjoying the less than 8% which it receives; of the inequities of taxation and tariff policies and their blighting effects upon agriculture, and of the whole train of hardships which these conditions have imposed upon farmers, upon rural society, and finally on the nation as a whole. The Master Farmers who have spoken, and Secretary Jardine, Professors Falconer, Lloyd, and others have shot these inescapable facts into the center of the pictue. We must frankly admit that the conference has not adequately answered the farmers' question, "How are those conditions to be overcome in order that the fuller life we seek may be realized"? At the same time it must be declared that this convention did not set itself to answer this question, but rather to throw light on the inter-relations existing between farm income and quality of life.

4. Emphasis has been placed on two inequalities which have their bases in legislation: the system of taxation which imposes a grossly disproportionate burden on real estate, and thus on farms, and on the tariff system. A revision of these systems, which would eliminate or at least reduce the maladjustments now existing, would not increase incomes but would release incomes for other needed purposes and they are factors in the situation. The load must be equalized. We have had much class legislation which has passed under the phraseology of the "general good." Tariff and taxation programs have tended to become class legislation. Inequity results when the successful economic group in the population dominates, as is usually the case.

5. Greater efficiency in production is not what we so much need now, but a more equitable distribution of wealth. Increased efficiency may conceivably accentuate the troubles rather than remedy them. Increased efficiency intensifies competition and lowers the level of profits. Furthermore, in agriculture the benefits of increased efficiency are diffused to consumers, not retained by farmers. *Equity in distribution transcends in importance the total income received.* On it hangs the sense of justice, the basis of contentment, and harmony among participating groups.

6. The greatest force in economic life today is the limiting of competition. Large businesses unite or cooperate to limit competi-

tion among them. Buyers of agricultural products resort to trade
agreements to restrict competition among them, which tends to force
farmers' prices up. By the same token farmers must adopt measures
to limit competition among themselves. They represent the greatest
body of competitors, to their own constant loss. Trade agreements
and cooperative action must be developed among farmers. So long
as the present unlimited competitive system continues, farmers will
not receive their equitable share of the national income.

7. There has been formulated, or at least given striking emphasis,
what to the country as a whole is essentially a new, and for once
adequate, definition of success in farming. Farming is a mode of life
as well as an occupation. It is a composite whole. It is at one and
the same time economic, social, physiological, psychological, or, if you
prefer, both human and material, in the satisfactions it demands.
Farm income and rate of return on invested capital, always important
and by some considered the primary, if not the sole criteria of success,
have been stated in their functional relationships with other com-
ponents of success.

8. Again, voice has here been given to a finer content of the
concept "standard of life," standard of living, or cultural level, as you
may prefer to call it. It is the sum total of values evolving from the
acquisition and from the use of goods and the use of time in the
satisfaction of human wants. This enriched concept affords a new
focal point for our thinking and for the direction of our energies.
It is a sort of mobilization center for all the working forces, economic,
sociological and psychological. It helps to set the parts in their proper
relation to the whole. It bids fair to clarify the goal of all rural endeavor, which will find its richest expression in a high standard of
living for increasing proportions of the population.

It is a contribution to progress when we clarify our thinking by
interpreting success in farming in terms of the standard of life sought
and the quality of life attained by the farm family, rather than merely
by financial returns.

9. Dr. H. C. Taylor has aptly pointed out that any class of
producers gets only what it consumes, and the farmers must learn
this lesson. Whether better income will be built into a better standard
of life depends upon the way the income is used. He urges that one
of the ways to improve the standard of life in the open country is for
farmers as a class to demand a better living and to refuse to farm
without it. This means that some will leave the farms; it also means
that increased income, instead of being generally used to acquire more
land to produce more crops or live-stock to make increased competition
which will lower prices and thus lower the level of living, will be in-

vested in part at least in those facilities and perquisites of a higher level which will yield satisfactions which make life pleasurable and efficient. This is a doctrine which has been little urged hitherto. Farmers will actually get only what they consume in economic, social, intellectual, and spiritual satisfactions.

The Secretary of Agriculture expressed a similar idea when he urged that more attention must be paid to having farmers achieve a higher efficiency in consumption, to seek the highest standard of life possible on their incomes. He would provide education in consumption values as well as in production and marketing values. How to consume the income becomes a major issue. It is not enough simply to consume more; one of the largest problems is how to use income so as to get the greatest value from such income as one has; how to get values such as other groups enjoy. There must be developed an adequate technique on how to utilize income. One must first get an income; he must then learn how to utilize it in terms of satisfactions; he must then consume it if he is to keep it. This is one of the clear pronouncements of the convention.

It must be admitted that this is a reversal of the traditional emphasis. It has been customary to urge the necessity for a larger income in order that the social and personal satisfactions may be acquired. There need be no fundamental conflict between the two modes of expression; but there is distinct value in now reversing the picture and setting out boldly that farmers really get only what they utilize, that their habits as consumers of economic and social goods need attention, and that they should demand higher standards of life as a groundwork for acquiring larger incomes. There are many inherent difficulties in acquiring the family and the community utilities which will make the satisfactions possible of realization, but the existence of an insistent demand will be a powerful aid.

This idea ties in very closely with one of the points brought out repeatedly in nearly all the groups which discussed the conference topic and whose reports you have just received. Whether one is discussing the relationship of education to income, or of health facilities, recreation, churches, household conveniences, or other utilities to income, nearly every group has voiced that the existence or the creation of the ideals, the desires for better utilities, is a prerequisite to their realization. What one wants sufficiently he is likely finally to obtain. While better education, for example, is in general correlated with better income, there is here a constant interplay of cause and effect. There is much evidence that the securing of an education is accomplished because of the individual's desire for it rather than because of economic status or nearness to schools. Such desire will frequently span the handicaps of distance or of poor economic status.

10.   The consciousness of community has been given a new emphasis. This applies in two quite diverse senses; in the community of interest of the workers in economics and in sociology; and in a larger sense in the functioning of rural communes as such. In many of the matters here discussed, the rural community is the unit through which, by concerted action, the ideals are to be realized. Communities which are real communes in consciousness, and are therefore cooperative in action, are most successfully realizing both economic competence and social satisfaction. In functional cooperation lies the roadway of achievement both of ideals and of the means for providing the utilities by which these ideals may be realized. There must be group actions and the pooling of interests, means, and powers in order to provide these larger satisfactions which are the very essence of an advancing civilization.

11.   Our national house is now divided into conflicting groups, rural and urban. Neither can finally be abstracted from the other. They are mutually contributory. The complementary relation of the two groups, always actual in fact, needs to be freed from mists of misunderstanding, indifference, even antagonism and perhaps exploitation, and seen afresh in the values which will result from a closer integration and a finer cooperation. It must be recognized that country life in America, whether approached from economic or cultural points of view, tends to be increasingly dominated by forces which originate in industrialized centers. The main features of city and rural culture finally merge. Recreation, religion, education, proceed toward a generalized pattern, and the city normally sets the pace whether we will it or not. City and country must devise means of living in mutually helpful relationships.

12.   The sociologist tells us that the human satisfactions which all persons seek are related to certain categories of their interests, namely, wealth, health, knowledge, beauty (or art), sociability, and righteousness. Progress for society is measured by an increased aggregate or juster proportion of these desirables or satisfactions for ever increasing number of the people. If we accept this general definition, may we not then harmonize our conceptions of farm income and farm life and of social justice into a single objective, and agree that agricultural progress is to be found in the process of achieving, on the part of people living on farms, in ever greater amount and juster proportion the higher levels of wealth, health, knowledge, beauty, sociability, and righteousness which we as a people have set as worthy of our loftiest desires and highest efforts. It is only by collective action that such progress will be realized.

13.   "Better farming, better business, and better living; and the

greatest of these is better living." If there is one pronouncement which has towered above others throughout these days of discussion, it is aptly expressed in these words.

PAST ISSUES AND FUTURE HOPES*

CARL C. TAYLOR,

Dean Graduate School North Carolina Agricultural College

The first National Country Life Conference was held at Baltimore in January 1919. This Conference dedicated itself to a survey of country life needs in America. In November of that year a second Conference was held at Chicago on the topic of Rural Health. Since then there has been a National Conference each year. In 1920 at Springfield, Mass., the topic was Rural Organization. In 1921 at New Orleans, Town-Country Relations; 1922 at New York, Rural Education; 1923, at St. Louis, The Rural Home; 1924, Columbus, Ohio, Religion in Country Life; 1925, Richmond, Va., Needed Adjustments in Rural Life; 1926, Washington, D. C., Rural Youth; 1927, East Lansing, Mich., Farm Income and Farm Life; in 1928, Urbana, Ill., Urban-Rural Relations.

At Baltimore in 1919 there was present 175 persons, representing 25 organizations. At East Lansing there were present 650 persons, representing 165 organizations.

In addition to holding the annual conferences the association publishes a monthly magazine, "Rural America." At the Conference meetings and in the publication many issues have been discussed by many people and agencies. Because it is not a legislative or administrative body or even a scientific body, there is no way of determining the absolute opinion of the association upon specific national issues and rural life policies. Because its members do not attempt to drive legislation or give promise of voting or bolting in blocks, the press of the country hasn't given particular attention to spreading the many significant view points that have been expressed in its meetings.

May I take your time, now therefore, to report some of the key notes of some of the meetings of the past. I shall not take time or pains to tell you just who said each of these things. Suffice it to tell you when and where each statement was made.

At Baltimore in 1919 the two following statements were made.

"One of the most effective methods of attaining agricultural

*From Address at Eleventh National Country Life Conference.

152

prosperity is to set in motion those great spiritual forces—education, co-operation, moral ideals—which give incentive for economic effort."

"The goal in country life organization is such an understanding and relationship of persons, forces and agencies, in a given area, whether community, county, state or nation, as will accomplish for that unit the most systematic and progressive correlation of those forces and agencies that make for sound development of a satisfactory life for rural people, and for the adjustment of their higher welfare and common good."

In the 1926 Meeting at Washington the following statement was made:

"It is more plain every day that the twentieth century type of city cannot be futher developed nor maintained without a twentieth century form of country life. The modern city is fortunately dependent on the country. And the American city especially so. No such great cities could have risen if the country had not furnished three-quarters of the people. In this country, foreign immigration gave additional members, and our cities boomed, as European cities never did. Today when this source is only a fraction of what it was, the cities must depend on rural emigrants or on their own natural increase. And such are their conditions and habits of life that they still draw two thirds of their growth from the country. Evidently the cities are in for a "slump" unless they change and improve their social conditions or take the leadership in a reconstruction of country life."

In 1927 at East Lansing, Michigan, the following statements were made:

"It must be recognized that country life in America, whether approached from economic or cultural points of view, tends to be increasingly dominated by forces which originate in industrial centers. The main features of city and rural culture finally merge. Recreation, religion, education, proceed toward a generalized pattern, and the city normally sets the pace whether we will it or not. City and country must devise means of living in mutually helpful relationships."

I have given these few quotations from past meetings to show how often and how truly the American Country Life Association has sounded notes of statesmanship on the abiding issues of rural life. I can't now take time for more than one or two such notes from this conference.

President Kinley said in his address of welcome:

"When great economic and social forces and economic and social classes are not in equilibrium, the problems incident thereto are more than class problems. They are national problems."

In this conference there have been held 14 sectional conferences and five platform meetings. As has been the case for the last five conferences scores of persons have participated, representing all kinds of agencies and institutions whose total time, energies and programs are dedicated to agricultural civilization and rural life in one way or another. It is impossible for me to bring together what has happened during these three days, for the reports, discussions and finding of the fourteen sections have not yet been mobilized. I dare say, however, that there has not been held in America this year a meeting which has deliberated upon and given expressions concerning as many important issues in agriculture and rural life as this conference has during these three days, not the Grange, the Farm Bureau, the Land Grant College Association, or Congress.

I believe that the two most significant things about this conference are: 1st, the bringing together of the urban and rural people and urban and rural interest,—though with the topic being what it is every one might well wish that more of the urban and industrial people had come; and 2nd, the presence of the great number of farmers and farm women—especially master farmers and master home-makers. At least a dozen times during this conference there has been thrown in the high light some such expression as this: "It is the *farm people themselves* and the agencies, institutions and organizations whose whole purpose and programs are dedicated to the solution of the problems and making of the policies of agriculture and rural life, *that must assume the leadership and dictate the destiny of this and all similar organizations.*

And now Mr. President may I be so audacious as to attempt to crystallize into expression a feeling and a hope which I think is brewing in the hearts and minds of many persons who are deeply concerned about the things with which this association is concerned.

I believe the time has come in American public sentiment and thinking when it is possible for some body of persons to furnish an agency by means of which something approaching as American agricultural policy can be tentatively formulated. The Land Grant College Association can't do it for we in the Association are technical experts, each pretty narrow in his field. Neither the Grange, the Farm Bureau nor the Farmers' Union can do it for they are separate bodies which seem to have difficulty in discovering common ground. The agricultural press can't do it for each agricultural paper is more or less a regional or state organ, largely dedicated to regional interest and problem. The volunteer agencies like the Y. M. C. A., Y. W. C. A., etc., can't do it for each has its highly specialized task. The American Country Life Asociation alone can do it. And I want to propose the following blue print for its immediate future.

First, that it settle the problem of whether it is a national or regional organization by becoming both; that it sponsor a National Annual Forum on Agricultural Issues and Agricultural Policies, and that it sponsor from five to seven Regional Country Life Conferences.

Second, that it foster the publication of a Journal of Rural Affairs, the mission of which will be to do continuously throughout the year the same thing that is done each year at the National Forum on Agricultural Issue and Policies and in the Regional Rural Life Conference, viz., develop a body of knowledge and philosophy of agriculture and rural life in America which will be wide spread and effective.

I am not proposing these steps as a "fly by night" suggestion. I have talked to dozens of prominent persons about these things—officers of the great farm organizations, leaders of the agricultural press, members of the official board of this association, friends of the American Country Life Association and outstanding leaders in the agricultural colleges of the country.

I am personally even more enthusiastic about the idea of a National Forum on Agricultural Issues and Policies than I am about the Regional Country Life Conferences, probably because this sort of thing has been shot at in one way or another from so many angles but never approached as a direct and specific project. I can not imagine a national meeting that would be attended more eagerly by the agricultural and even industrial leaders of the country, or covered more enthusiastically by the press than a Forum this year, let's say, on Agricultural Relief. I believe that such a Forum would be of equal significance, interest and importance to the Williamstown meeting on International Affairs. The leaders of great farmers organizations that now get together only incidentally and from time to time at congressional hearings would come together in frank and above board deliberation. The technical agricultural expert would meet the leaders of these practical farmers' organizations. The different sections of the country would all be represented. The industrial and commercial leaders would not fail to be there. The leaders of the more socially and idealistically minded agencies, the farm economist and rural sociologist, would be heard, not only by their own fellow spirits but by those whom they most desire to reach. The national and state official representatives of agriculture would be met at such a meeting by all these other representatives. I simply cannot vision such a gathering without the greatest enthusiasm. I think it lies within the genius of the American Country Life Association as it does not within the genius of any other organization or association in America to establish this institution.

I wonder if I have made the picture clear—a picture not constructed by myself alone, but one which has been evolving rather slowly and naturally for the last few years, some elements in which the board has discussed and all of which was finally thrown together during mid-night sessions of the conference. Concretely the picture is of an American Country Life Association which operates as the sponsor for four great projects: (1) Five or six Regional Country Life Conferences covering the whole nation and conducted within reach and by the help of the people in the regions; (2) A National Forum on Agricultural Issues and Policies, participated in by the organizational, institutional, intellectual, political and practical agri-agricultural leaders of the nation; (3) The publication of a Journal of Rural Affairs, it also being a forum on agricultural issue and policies. (4) The reviving and development of the National Council of Rural Social Agencies.

OFFICERS AND COMMITTEES - 1928

OFFICERS

KENYON L. BUTTERFIELD, *President*, East Lansing, Michigan.

MRS. C. C. SCHUTTLER, *Vice-President*, Farmington, Missouri.

WALTER J. CAMPBELL, *Chairman Executive Committee*, Springfield, Massachusetts.

NAT T. FRAME, *Executive Secretary*, Waddington Farm, Wheeling, W. Va.

BENSON Y. LANDIS, *Editor "Rural America"*, 105 E. 22nd St., New York City.

ALBERT SHAW, JR., *Treasurer*, 55 Fifth Ave., New York City.

BOARD OF DIRECTORS

One Year Term—Expiring 1929

KENYON L. BUTTERFIELD, East Lansing Michigan.

CHARLES F. JENKINS, Philadelphia, Pennsylvania.

FRANK O. LOWDEN, Oregon, Illinois.

EDWIN V. O'HARA, Eugene, Oregon.

MRS. CHARLES C. SCHUTTLER, Farmington, Missouri.

C. B. SMITH, Washington, D. C.

L. J. TABER, Columbus, Ohio.

Two Year Term—Expiring 1930.

EDMUND DES. BRUNNER, New York, N. Y.

NAT T. FRAME, Morgantown, W. Va.

A. R. MANN, Ithaca, N. Y.

R. K. BLISS, Ames, Iowa.

MRS. A. H. REEVE, Ambler, Pennsylvania.

ALBERT SHAW, JR., New York.

C. C. TAYLOR, Raleigh, North Carolina.

Three Year Term—Expiring 1931.

W. J. CAMPBELL, Springfield, Massachusetts.

MISS MABEL CARNEY, New York, N. Y.

E. C. LINDEMAN, New York, N. Y.

Henry Morgenthau, Jr., New York, N. Y.

G. I. CHRISTIE, Guelph, Ontario, Canada.

HENRY C. TAYLOR, Burlington, Vermont.

MRS. KATHRYN VAN AKEN BURNS, Urbana, Illinois.

STUDENT REPRESENTATIVES

WM. H. TUFTS, East Lansing, Michigan.
HERMAN BOWERS, Morgantown, W. Va.

FIELD REPRESENTATIVE

HENRY ISRAEL, New York N. Y.

COMMITTEES

EXECUTIVE, Walter J. Campbell, *Chairman.*

Henry Morgenthau, Jr., Mabel Carney, Charles F. Jenkins, A. R. Mann, Edmund deS. Bruner, Albert Shaw, Jr.

RURAL ORGANIZATION, Murl McDonald, *Chairman*, Ames, Iowa.

C. V. Gregory, Prairie Farmer, Chicago, Ill., Eben Mumford, Michigan Agricultural College, East Lansing, Mich., C. C. Burns, Champaign, Ill., Dan A. Wallace, Minneapolis, Minn., B. L. Hummell, University of Missouri, Columbia, Mo., Walter Burr, Kansas Agricultural College, Manhattan, Kansas, Gertrude Humphreys, Morgantown, W. Va., Perry P. Denune, Ohio State University, Columbus, Ohio, Miss Neale S. Knowles, Ames, Iowa, J. R. Hutcheson, Blacksburg, Va., Clarence Henry, Indianapolis, Ind., C. E. Allred, University of Tennessess, N. R. Kibler, American Farm Bureau Federation, Chicago, Ill., Ralph A. Felton, Cornell University, Ithaca, N. Y., T. R. Bryant, Extension Division, Lexington, Ky., A. D. McLarty, Municipal League, Urbana, Ill., H. C. Ramsower, Ohio State University, Columbus, Ohio, S. B. Cleland, University of Minnesota, Minneapolis, Minn., L. L. Meedler, Secretary Farm Bureau, Indianapolis, Ind., M. J. Kreisle, Tell City, Ind., H. F. Link, Lexington, Ky., D. P. Trent, Stillwater, Okla., Dr. C. C. Schuttler, Farmington, Mo., O. W. Beeler, Des Moines, Iowa, Mr. William Van Bloom, Dayton, Iowa.

COMMUNITY SCORE CARDS, Aubrey Williams, *Chairman*, Madison, Wisc.

C. E. Stockdale, Extension Division, Morgantown, W. Va., W. H. Stacy, Iowa State, Ames, Iowa, E. P. Taylor, American Farming, Chicago, Ill., Dr. E. H. Lauer, Iowa City, Iowa, W. E. Garnett, V. P. I., Blacksburg, Va., J. E. Wilson, County Agent, Williamstown, Ky., F. G. Hall, County Agent, Wilmington, Ohio, J. A. Dickey, University of Arkansas, Fayetteville, Ark., Dr. C. R. Mann, Council of Education, Washington, D. C., Mrs. Ethel S. Morgan, Ames, Iowa, Clarence E. Ridley, Syracuse University, Syracuse, New York, George A. Starring, Huron, South Dakota, Donald R. Murphy, Des Moines, Iowa, H. M. Armstrong, Norman, Okla., B. L. Hummel, Agricultural College, Columbia, Mo., R. S. Rauschkolb, St. Louis, Mo.

COMMUNITY PLANNING, Lee F. Hanmer, *Chairman*, Russell Sage Foundation, N. Y.

Thomas Adams, Russell Sage Foundation, New York, N. Y., C. C. Colby, University of Chicago, Chicago, Ill., Frank A. Waugh, Massachusetts Agricultural College, Amherst, Mass., F. A. Aust, University of Wisconsin, Madison, Wis., A. L. Peck, Oregon State College, Corvallis, Oregon, Miss Harlean James, Union Trust Building, Washington, D. C., Dr. L. C. Gray, U. S. Dept. of Agriculture, Washington, D. C., Crispin Oglebay, Cleveland, Ohio, Robert Kingery, Burnham Building, Chicago, Ill., Julia D. Connor, Better Homes in America, Washington, D. C., Shirley Allen, American Forestry Association, Washington, D. C., John D. Willard, Michigan State College, East Lansing, Mich., Elwood Street, The Community Council, St. Louis, Mo., Julia Rocheford, University of Missouri, Columbia, Mo., Sybil Burton, 3424 Rowlanas Bldg., Columbus, Ohio, Mrs. H. G. Sturm, Clarksburg, W. Va., M. S. Smith,

Bluffton, Ind., Jesse E. Whonsetler, Bucyrus, Ohio, T. A. McNeal, Topeka Kansas, Henry W. A. Rott, Pres. St. Louis Co. Farm Bureau, Afton, Mo., L. J. Murphy, Ames, Iowa, T. H. Alwood, Ames, Iowa, John Nolen, Cambridge, Mass., Sam Jordan, Sedalia, Mo., C. L. Burkholder, Lafayette, Ind., Walter Kohler, Kohler, Wis., Leonard R. Condon, Rockford, Ill., Lawrence Sheridan, Indianapolis, Ind., F. Herbert Hare, 114 W. Tenth St., Kansas City, Mo., Jacob Crane, Chicago, Ill.

TOWN-COUNTRY COOPERATION, R. K. BLISS, *Chairman*, Ames, Iowa

C. C. Zimmerman, University of Minnesota, Minneapolis, Minn., J. B. Reynolds, Ontario Agricultural College, Guelph, Ontario, Canada, L. J. Taber, Master National Grange, Columbus, Ohio, Florence E. Ward, U. S. Department of Agriculture, Washington, D. C., Harper Dean, U. S. Chamber of Commerce, Washington, D. C., Daniel H. Otis, American Bankers Association, Madison, Wis., Frank H. Jeter, Kiwanis International, Raleigh, N. C., Miss Sybil Burton, 3424 Rowlanas Avenue, Columbus, Ohio, Mrs. Spencer Ewing, Bloomington, Ill., Ward R. Miles, University of Oklahoma, Norman, Okla., Chas. E. Gunnels, Moline, Ill., E. E. Faville, Portland, Oregon, Fred Murphy, Tribune, Minneapolis, Minn., Anne Hinrichson, 231 La Salle Street, Chicago, Ill., Carl Vrooman, Bloomington, Ill., E. S. Bayard, Stockman and Farmer, Pittsburgh, Pa., Mrs. Ingram, Quincy, Ill., Mrs. Wm. Cottrill, Des Moines, Iowa, R # 6, Wm. A. McArthur, Mason City. Iowa, Mason Yerkes, State Agent, Lincoln, Neb., F. B. Stitt, El Paso, Ill., T. J. Talbert, Columbia, Mo., R. W. Brown, Carrolltown, Mo., Walter Wadsworth, Editor, Farm Club News, Springfield, Mo., Edward Bruder, President Missouri Bankers Association, Mercantile Trust Co., St. Louis, Mo.

RURAL GOVERNMENT, John A. Fairlie, *Chairman*, Urbana, Ill.

T. B. Manny, U. S. Department of Agriculture, Washington, D. C., C. L. Stewart, University of Illinois, Urbana, Ill., Benjamin F. Shambaugh, University of Iowa, Des Moines, Iowa, Griff Johnson, Vice-Pres., Iowa Equitable Life Ins. Co., Des Moines, Iowa, R. H. Gist, Morgantown, W. Va., E. C. Branson, University of North Carolina, Chapel Hill, N. C., E. H. Ryder, Michigan Agricultural College, East Lansing, Mich., W. L. Bailey, Northwestern University, Evanston, Ill., Miss Elliott, Teachers College, Greensboro, N. C., Mayo Fesler, Cleveland, Ohio, Bertha C. Bidwell, Freeport, Ill., Minnie Price, Columbus, Ohio, Mrs. Chas. W. Sewall, Otterbein, Ind., Mrs. L. E. Johnson, Farmington, Mo., Miss Ina Taylor, Iowa City, Iowa, D. C. Wood, College of Agriculture, Columbia, Mo., C. O. Brannon, University of Arkansas, Fayetteville, Ark., L. B. Schmidt, Ames, Iowa, L. B. Palmer, Ohio Farm Bureau, Columbus, Ohio, Xenophon Caverno, Canalou, Mo.

RURAL HEALTH, C. E. Lively, *Chairman*, Columbus, Ohio.

Dr. L. L. Lunsden, U. S. Public Health Service, Washington, D. C., Dr. Walter A. Brown, Child Health Demonstration, Salem, Oregon, Dr. Blanche M. Haines, Children's Bureau, Washington, D. C., Miss Fanny Dunn, Teachers College, New York, N. Y., Dr. W. T. Henshaw, State Health Com., Charleston, W. Va., Edna L. Foley, Chicago, Dr. H. H. Moore, American Medical Association, Washington, D. C., Emma Doefinger, Child Health Association, New York, N. Y., Dr. W. H. Ramsey, Farmer's Wife, St. Paul, Minn., Fanny M. Brooks, University of Illinois, Urbana, Ill., Dr. Grace S. Wightman, Springfield, Ill., Dr. William F. King, Secretary Board of Health, Indianapolis, Ind., Mrs. Jane Kerr, Secretary, Ill. T. B. & P. H. Ass'n, Springfield, Ill., Dr. Henry Albert, Des Moines, Iowa, Dr. C. L. Wendt, Canton, S. Dak., Miss Mary E. Stebbins, Columbia, Mo., Miss Pearle McIvor, Jefferson City, Mo.

RURAL SCHOOLS, Mrs. Katherine M. Cook, *Chairman*, Washington, D. C.

Dr. M. S. Pittman, State Teachers College, Ypsilanti, Mich., Miss Helen H. Heyl,

160   OFFICERS AND COMMITTEES

Department of Education, State Capital, Albany, N. Y., Mr. W. C. Nason, Washington, D. C., Amalia M. Bengtson, New York, U. J. Hoffman, State Department of Education, State Capital, Springfield, Ill., Pres. C. C. Swain, State Teachers College, Mayville, S. Dak., R. C. Moore, Carlinville, Ill., Miss Marion Humble, 25 W. 33rd Street, New York, N. Y., Miss Anna May Price, Springfield, Ill., Mr. Thomas J. Smart, University of Kansas, Lawrence, Kansas, Z. M. Smith, Lafayette, Ind., Mr. W. McK. Robinson, Western Teachers College, Kalamazoo, Mich., Miss Mabel Carney, Teachers College, Columbia University, New York City, Miss Agnes Samuelson, State Supt., Des Moines, Iowa, W. H. Lancelot, Ames, Iowa, Alson Secor, Des Moines, Iowa, E. C. Wissler, County Supt., Boone, Iowa, Charles A. Lee, State Supt., Jefferson City. Mo., Elizabeth White, Maryville, Mo.

RURAL CHURCH, Samuel A. Guard, *Chairman,* Chicago, Ill.

Ralph S. Adams, 1505 Race Street, Philadelphia, Pa., Edwin V. O'Hara, National Catholic Welfare Conference, Eugene, Oregon, Gabriel Davidson, Jewish Agricultural Society, 301 E. 14th St., New York City, Malcolm Dana, 287 Fourth Avenue, New York City, Arthur E. Holt, University of Chicago, Chicago, Ill., Paul F. Sanders, Orland, Ill., James Speed, Southern Agriculturist, Louisville, Ky., Bishop Edwin N. Hughes, Chicago, Ill., Miss Adria Titterington, National Board Y. W. C. A., Chicago, Ill., M. A. Dawber, Methodist Board of Home Missions, 1701 Arch St., Philadelphia, Pa., Warren H. Wilson, 156 Fifth Avenue, New York City, A. H. Rapking, Weston, W. Va., Carl Hutchinson, 5757 University Ave., Chicago, Ill., Dr. C. A. Barbour, 151 Saratoga Ave., Rochester, N. Y., Rev. C. A. Shake, R. F. D., Evansville, Ind., Mrs. W. W. Henderson, La Plata, Mo., Rev. Chas. W. Estes, Rolia, Mo., A. E. Fish, Osage, Iowa, R. J. Montgomery, Grinnell, Iowa, C. N. Bigelow, Adel, Iowa, Rev. Herman Taylor, Pilot Grove, Mo., Rev. F. A. Wangelin, Grandin, Mo., Father George Hildner, Claryville, Mo.

RURAL LEADERSHIP TRAINING, E. L. Morgan, *Chairman,* Columbia, Mo.

George C. Works, University of Chicago, Chicago, Ill., E. H. Shinn, Department of Agriculture, Washington, D. C., Dean W. C. Coffee, University of Minnesota, St. Paul, Minn., Dean Alfred Vivian, Ohio State University, Columbus, Ohio, Rev. H. W. McLaughlin, Box 1176, Richmond, Va., Lita Bane, University of Wisconsin, Madison, Wis., Ruth A. Wardell, University of Illinois, Urbana, Ill., Edna N. White, Merrell-Palmer School, Detroit, Mich., W. J. Hutchins, Pres, of Berea College, Berea, Ky., H. W. Shryock, Southern Illinois Normal University, Carbondale, Ill., Chas, A. Lory, Ft. Collins, Colo., W. D. Nicholls, University of Kentucky, Lexington, Ky., Edw. M. Tuttle, Chicago, Ill., Alma L. Binzel, Chicago, Ill., A. B. Graham, Extension Service, Washington, D. C., M. P. Shawley, Pres. of Marshall College, Huntington, W. Va., D. L. Noble, Boys and Girls Club Committee, Chicago, Ill., David A. Robertson, 26 Jackson Place, Washington, D. C., Moses A. Cartwright, Association of Adult Education, New York City, Grace E. Freysinger, Dept, of Agriculture, Washington, D. C., J. Earl Romine, Wheeling, W. Va., Mrs. A. W. Errett, Kewanee, Ill., J. M. Artman, Sec'y Religious Education Ass'n, 308 N. Mich. Ave., Chicago, Ill., O. H. Benson, Dept. Rural Scouting, 200 5th Ave., New York City, H. A. Klahr, Sec'y C. E. Union, 511 Clinton Bldg., Columbus, Ohio, John B. Foster, Ames, Iowa, Paul Barker, Ames, Iowa, Bird C. Baldwin, Iowa City, Iowa, C. H. Lane, 200 N. J. Ave., Washington, D. C., J. E. Kirkpatrick, Olivet, Mich., Mrs. F. C. Beverly, Whitmell, Va., A. J. Meyers, Columbia, Mo.

FARM INCOME AND FARM LIFE, H. C. Taylor, *Chairman,* Evanston, Ill.

John H. Kolb, University of Wisconsin, Madison, Wis., O. G. Lloyd, Purdue University, Lafayette, Ind., Dwight Sanderson, Cornell University, Ithaca, N, Y., E. G. Nourse, Institute of Economics, Washington, D. C., Geneva Bain, University of

Wisconsin, Madison, Wis., Arthur Huntington, Cedar Rapids, Iowa, F. Roger Miller, Asheville, N. C., Everett Porter, Bedford, Ind., Scott Doup, Columbus, Ind., Luther Fuller, Danville, Ill., Carl Williams, Oklahoma City, Okla., T. J. Delohery, 110 E. Dearborn Street, Chicago, Ill., S. H. Thompson, American Farm Bureau Federation, Chicago, Ill., E. A. Eckert, Mascoutah, Ill., Melvin A. Traylor, Chicago, Ill., Julian Friant, Cape Girardeau, Mo., Chas. H. McDowell, Armour Fert Works, Chicago, Ill., Mary T. Barber, Battle Creek, Mich., Alex. Legge, 365 S. Michigan Avenue, Chicago. Ill., P. H. Ward, Farm Journal, Philadelphia, Pa., Miss Aubyn Chinn, National Dairy Council, 985 S. Michigan Avenue, Chicago, Ill., True D. Morse,3223 Washington Boulevard, St. Louis, Mo., W. B. Weisenburger, NationalBank of Commerce, St. Louis, Mo.